Teaching with Compassion

Teaching with Compassion

An Educator's Oath to Teach from the Heart

Peter Kaufman
Janine Schipper

ROWMAN & LITTLEFIELD
Lanham • Boulder • New York • London

Published by Rowman & Littlefield
An imprint of The Rowman & Littlefield Publishing Group, Inc.
4501 Forbes Boulevard, Suite 200, Lanham, Maryland 20706
www.rowman.com

Unit A, Whitacre Mews, 26-34 Stannary Street, London SE11 4AB

British Library Cataloguing in Publication Information Available

Library of Congress Cataloging-in-Publication Data

Names: Kaufman, Peter, 1967– author. | Schipper, Janine, 1970– author.
Title: Teaching with compassion : an educator's oath to teach from the heart / Peter Kaufman, Janine Schipper.
Description: Lanham : Rowman & Littlefield Publishing Group, Inc., [2018] | Includes bibliographical references and index.
Identifiers: LCCN 2018012108 (print) | LCCN 2018018766 (ebook) | ISBN 9781475836561 (ebook) | ISBN 9781475836547 (cloth : alk. paper) | ISBN 9781475836554 (pbk. : alk. paper)
Subjects: LCSH: Reflective teaching. | Buddhism and education. | Teacher-student relationships.
Classification: LCC LB1027.22 (ebook) | LCC LB1027.22 .K38 2018 (print) | DDC 371.102—dc23
LC record available at https://lccn.loc.gov/2018012108

∞™ The paper used in this publication meets the minimum requirements of American National Standard for Information Sciences—Permanence of Paper for Printed Library Materials, ANSI/NISO Z39.48-1992.

Printed in the United States of America

Peter wishes to dedicate this book to Leigh: *If I were just an I it would be more difficult to be me than when I am part of us.*

Janine wishes to dedicate this book to her mentor, Maury Stein, a teacher whose powerful compassionate presence has served as a remarkable model throughout her life.

Contents

Preface

If you are reading this book, it is likely that you care about students, about the people you work with, and about the schools that you work in. It is also likely that as a teacher you have experienced frustration—even anger—from time to time. And sometimes you may feel at your wits' end.

Perhaps you have observed a growing number of students struggling emotionally and academically, or you have felt an increase in pressure to perform more with less. Or maybe you have felt the dehumanizing effects of increased bureaucratization and standardization of the educational system. Many reading this book may find themselves overworked and rundown, in search of ways to reconnect with the precious golden seed that brought you to teaching in the first place.

Whether you are new to teaching or are an experienced educator, we wish to acknowledge your commitment and dedication to the profession. We know and appreciate that the readers of this book value the craft of teaching and are seeking tools and strategies to connect with and help students. As teachers who also care deeply for students and the people and institutions in which we work, we wrote this book as part of our own journeys as educators.

Nearly twenty years ago, the United Nations Educational, Scientific, and Cultural Organization (UNESCO) published "What Makes a Good Teacher?"—a study based on children's responses from fifty countries. The overwhelming answer to the question of what makes a good teacher was compassion. The director-general of UNESCO summed up the students' responses in this way: "There is only one pedagogy, the pedagogy of love."[1]

One might think, naively, that since the publication of this report, love might have become a popular buzzword of the educational world. Instead, the conversations about how to make schools better, both in the popular media and among education professionals and researchers, rarely consist of proposals for teachers to treat students with greater care, concern, kindness, and love. Most teacher education curriculums focus on neither love nor compassion; rather, the emphasis is on content areas, learning strategies, cognitive development, assessment, curriculum development, educational technologies, theory and methods, and practical classroom experience.[2]

In fact, a recent search of the EBSCO database ERIC (Educational Resources Information Center) yielded only one result in the last twenty years for the phrase "teaching with compassion" and zero results for "teach with compassion." Similar searches for "teach (and teaching) with kindness," "teach (and teaching) with love," and "teach (and teaching) with empathy" similarly yielded few, if any, results.

Even in the increasingly popular and broad field of social and emotional learning (SEL), compassion and kindness are not always prominently discussed. In a recent comprehensive report of the SEL literature and a strong call for its incorporation into school curriculums, compassion, while arguably implied throughout the report, was only mentioned once and kindness was not mentioned at all.[3]

In those instances when compassion is part of the conversation, there seems to be an assumption that if one can teach students how to be compassionate, then one knows how to be a compassionate educator. But this assumption is not always true. Just as there are health care providers with unhealthy lifestyles and lawyers who stretch the truth, there are educators who teach about compassion but struggle with teaching *with* compassion.

For some, the idea that education could improve by teachers opening up their hearts and minds may seem naive, impractical, or even wrongheaded. In an educational environment focused on high standards, rigor, and grit, is there a place for teachers to be accepting and understanding? We would argue that there is.

Indeed, we would go so far as to assert that rigor without compassion is a risky enterprise, setting students up for failure rather than success. Teaching with compassion is not an *alternative* to the educational focus on achievement and outcomes; rather, it is a baseline orientation from which all educators may begin their work.

The argument that if we are overly kind and generous toward students we will be taken advantage of and students will not learn is not confirmed by any research. In fact, the growing body of research on compassion demonstrates quite clearly that when we act with compassion three things occur: we thrive, others thrive, and communities thrive.[4] In other words, if we teach with compassion our teaching will improve and be more satisfying, our students will perform and feel better, and our schools will be more welcoming and inviting.

At the most basic level, *Teaching with Compassion* offers educators a rationale and a blueprint for teaching with kindness, generosity, care, and concern for *all* students. The book is based on practices that enable us to relinquish our egocentric orientations and direct our energies toward the care of others. We encourage teachers at all levels and in all educational institutions to contemplate the two most important and interconnected relationships in the educational process: our relationship with ourselves and our relationship with students.

By emphasizing this connectedness we are better able to teach from the heart. Parker Palmer, whose work is a constant source of influence and inspiration for us, makes this point in *The Courage to Teach*: "The connections made by good teachers are held not in their methods but in their hearts—meaning *heart* in its ancient sense, as the place where intellect and emotion and spirit will converge in the human self."[5]

All educators are well trained in following curriculum guides, learning standards, and accrediting dictates. *Teaching with Compassion* asks that you also follow your innate "compassionate instinct."[6] To this end, our goal is to provide educators with a foundation and a set of strategies to allow this natural inclination to flourish so that the power and potential it offers will be clearly evident.

We know that many readers of this book already prioritize teaching with compassion and spend a lot of time and energy developing and fostering compassion in the classroom. *Teaching with Compassion* offers those already committed to the path of compassionate teaching further opportunities for reflection as well as suggestions for deepening their inquiry into how to address challenges, facilitate active and experiential learning, and cultivate a community of learners and a more humanizing educational experience.

We are both professors of sociology—one of us at the State University of New York at New Paltz, a midsize public liberal arts college, and the other at Northern Arizona University, a larger public research university. In over forty years of combined teaching experience, we have encountered thousands of undergraduates from across the globe—albeit, the majority of students have hailed from the United States, and most have come from the respective states in which we teach.

For both of us, the desire to write this book grew out of a shared commitment to making the educational process kinder and more openhearted. To paraphrase the oft-quoted advice from Mahatma Gandhi, we want to be the compassionate educators we wish to see in this world.

This orientation emanates from three primary influences: sociology, critical pedagogy, and Buddhism. Sociology provides the analytical impulse to identify problems in the educational process, including our own culpability in these problems, and then seek ways to improve them. Critical pedagogy offers a humanistic and change-oriented educational model. And Buddhism presents the philosophical underpinnings of compassion, practices to foster its growth, and insights to understand and ultimately relieve suffering.

We both share a strong compulsion to put compassion into practice throughout all aspects of our lives. Much of this approach comes from years of meditation practice while simultaneously studying and teaching sociology. Through these endeavors, we began to see the extent and depth of suffering within ourselves, within others, and throughout the world.

Teaching with compassion is central to our work as educators but it is always a work in progress. Writing a book about teaching with compassion is both a means for us to share what we have learned over the years and also a way to continue the ongoing endeavor of cultivating compassion in the classroom and throughout other dimensions of academic life.

In writing *Teaching with Compassion*, we have gained a greater understanding of and appreciation for what it means to become more compassionate teachers. We acknowledge that we still have much to learn, but we appreciate being on this path. We extend our gratitude to you, the reader, for taking this journey into teaching with compassion with us!

Acknowledgments

You are a creator of your own garden. Plant kindness and compassion.
Water with love and gratitude. And you will enjoy beauty all the days of
your life.

—Julie Parker

The whole idea of compassion is based on a keen awareness of the inter-
dependence of all these living beings, which are all part of one another,
and all involved in one another.

—Thomas Merton

Compassion and gratitude. It's hard to imagine one without the other. When we act with compassion we are reaching out to others, working with them to relieve their suffering, ease their burden, or help them along the path. When we offer gratitude to others we do so because they have reached out to us, worked with us to relieve our suffering, eased our burden, or helped us along the path.

This book would not be possible without others showing compassion to us. During the course of writing this book, as well as the many years that preceded it, we sought assistance, guidance, direction, or just company from countless individuals. Their efforts, their nurturing, and their compassion have given us the space and the opportunities to write *Teaching with Compassion*. Here we take the opportunity to water with love and gratitude all those who have allowed us to embark upon and complete this journey.

To the thousands of students with whom we have had the privilege to teach and learn over the course of our teaching careers—we obviously can't list you all by name but we hope you know that this book is both because of you and ultimately for you. Through your openness, honesty, and perseverance, you have shown us what compassion is and why it is so crucial to the educational process.

Many educators read and offered feedback on sections of this manuscript. The critical but compassionate feedback they offered pushed us to rethink our assumptions, recognize and address our blind spots, and guard against our occasional forays into academese. We acknowledge that any shortcomings of the book are our own, but we know the book is stronger and more appealing to a wider audience because of your efforts. Thank you, Alex Alvarez, Karen Ball, Gregory Bynum, Deborah Cohan, Damien Contessa, Becky Dimick Eastman, Lynette Liberge, Mara Pfeffer, Tina Skuce, Pamela Vivanco, and Randall Wisehart.

Our colleagues and dear friends continually shape us as thinkers, teachers, writers, and human beings. Many of them will no doubt be familiar with the ideas in this book as they have sprung forth from the conversations, reflections, and even disagreements we have shared over the years. They have regularly inquired about and were kept appraised of the book's progress on walks, hikes, and bike rides; during meals; and at gatherings. We know that you are as excited to see this book completed as we are. Your input, encouragement, and enthusiasm have been contagious and have helped us maintain the flame of productivity.

Peter sends gratitude to Susan Blickstein, Patrica Carson, Mette Christiansen, James Dembowski, Judy Dorney, Glenn Geher, Giorgio Melloni, Maureen Morrow, Terry Murray, Brian Obach, Thomas Olsen, Ilgu Ozler, Jonathan Perl, Todd Schoepflin, Barry Shapiro, Kathryn Stewart, Ann Ward, and Michael Ziebell. Janine sends gratitude to Shannon Arnett, Karla Hackstaff, Yvonne Luna, Aleia O'Reilly, Diedra Silbert, Cathy Small, and the entire Further Shore family, who have taught her what it truly means to be a part of a community of care and compassion.

We would also like to extend our gratitude to the nurses, doctors, and other health care professionals who have kept us healthy as we dealt with some unexpected bumps along the way. Your actions have modeled for us the Hippocratic Oath on which our own Teaching with Compassion Oath is based. Witnessing and experiencing your compassion in action has been comforting in times of suffering and inspirational in times of writing.

We are especially grateful to have found and worked with Paula Stacey, whose professional editing skills and insight helped us hone in on key messages. Alana Minkler helped each oath point come alive through her ingenious and inspired illustrations. And the staff at Rowman & Littlefield, particularly our editor, Sarah Jubar, demonstrated enthusiasm for the project every step of the way and were fully supportive when we needed to extend the timeline.

We are ever grateful for the love and support of our families.

Peter offers endless gratitude to his parents, Toby and Barry Kaufman, and his brothers and their families—Jonathan Kaufman, Milissa Hicks, and Una Hicks-Kaufman, and Joshua Kaufman, Greg Gibson, and Julia Gibson-Kaufman—for their unwavering love and support. Peter also thanks Leigh Weaver, his lifelong partner in love and friendship and his daily reminder of what it means to truly teach with and live with compassion; this book would not be possible without her.

Janine thanks her beloved partner, Eliot, for his boundless heart, wisdom, and ceaseless support. Eliot and her three children are Janine's inspiration, their presence a continual reminder to breathe and experience the aliveness of the present moment. Janine also thanks her parents, Barbara and Larry Berkowitz, whose endless love and care have provided a foundation for all that she does.

Introduction

What Is Compassion?

Compassion is the radicalism of our time.

—Dalai Lama

One day a man was walking on a beach and he came upon a young girl. He couldn't quite see what she was doing, but it looked like she was picking something up in the sand and then throwing it gently into the ocean. "Good morning," the man called out, "what are you doing there?" The young girl looked up at the man and said, "I'm throwing these starfish back into the ocean." "Why are you throwing starfish into the ocean?" the man asked. The girl looked at the man again and replied, "The tide is on its way out. If these starfish do not get back into the ocean they will soon die."

The man scanned the entire sea shore and became noticeably perplexed. He said to the girl, "But there are hundreds of starfish along this stretch of beach. You can't possibly make a difference by just tossing a few starfish back into the ocean." Hearing what the man said the girl picked up a starfish and tossed it into the ocean: "I made a difference for that one."

This tale, or versions of it, often finds its way into popular speeches and workshops. Based on a story within a classic essay by naturalist, philosopher, and scholar Loren Eiseley called "The Star Thrower," it contains many themes and lessons; however, at its core it is a story of compassion, an account of how, in the course of our everyday existence, we can take steps to relieve the pain and suffering of others.[1]

As Buddhist teacher Judith Lief suggests, this sort of compassionate action is fundamental to who we are: "Compassion is inherent in our very nature as human beings. It is natural to us. We do not need to create it. Cultivating compassion does not mean injecting some new, improved element into ourselves so that we can work more effectively. Instead, we simply uncover the compassion that is already there."[2]

Too often, however, we may think of compassion as something that only a few, saint-like people can achieve. Or we may believe we can only be compassionate after a long, arduous spiritual journey. We regularly point out the compassionate acts of others with a sense of awe and reverence: *If only I could be like that.* But the truth is we *are* all like that. Compassion is very much part of our basic human nature. There is nothing extraordinary about those who exhibit compassion in their daily lives; they are simply acting human. But they are also making a choice.

The evolutionary biologist Stephen Jay Gould argues that "violence, sexism, and general nastiness *are* biological since they represent one subset of a possible range of behaviors. But peacefulness, equality, and kindness are just as biological—and we may see their influence increase if we can create social structures that permit them to flourish."[3]

The question, then, is what aspects of our human nature do we encourage and promote? Even if we accept that compassion is part of our DNA, that indeed "we are hardwired for compassion" as Christopher Kukk points out in *The Compassionate Achiever*,[4] we need to know it and understand it if we want to promote it. So, what does it mean to be compassionate?

THE DIMENSIONS OF COMPASSION

While compassion is central to nearly every religious, spiritual, and ethical school of thought and it has been defined by countless scholars, philosophers, and religious traditions, the essence of true compassion, how to make it real in our lives every day, can be elusive.

Bringing compassion to our daily lives is an effort that is getting global attention, in particular via the work of religious scholar and bestselling author Karen Armstrong. Having won the TED prize for her influential work in 2008, she used her winnings as a springboard to call upon the world to create a Charter for Compassion. Unveiled in 2009, the Charter for Compassion is a 312-word pledge developed from contributions of more than 150,000 people from 180 countries.

So, while our discussions and insights throughout this book have been informed by many spiritual teachers, educational research, and our own experience, it makes sense to begin our search for understanding compassion with insights from Karen Armstrong's book, *Twelve Steps to a Compassionate Life.* Through her twelve steps, she encourages people to do the following, among other things:[5]

- Always treat all others as we wish to be treated ourselves
- Work tirelessly to alleviate the suffering of our fellow creatures
- Dethrone ourselves from the center of our world and put another there
- Honor the inviolable sanctity of every single being
- Treat everybody, without exception, with absolute justice, equity, and respect
- Refrain consistently and emphatically from inflicting pain
- Do not deny our common humanity by: acting or speaking violently out of spite, chauvinism or self-interest; impoverishing, exploiting or denying basic rights to anybody; and inciting hatred by denigrating others—even our enemies

Armstrong emphasizes that there are many dimensions of what it means to act, or in our case, teach, with compassion. There is no single way to be compassionate nor is there a readily available template that we can apply to all situations. Different circumstances and settings may bring about different acts of compassion. We can teach compassionately with our words, actions, behaviors, gestures, expectations, and even our thoughts. Sometimes we may even teach with compassion through our silence. In fact, every encounter and experience we have is an opportunity to practice compassion in some capacity.

COMPASSION VERSUS EMPATHY

While compassion is multifaceted, it isn't simply a broad concept that holds everything nice and good. It is important to be clear about what it is and isn't. An important distinction should be made, for example, between compassion and empathy, as the two terms often get used interchangeably. Empathy is the capacity to place oneself in another's shoes, to experience what the other is experiencing. When we exhibit empathy, we take on another person's frame of reference and allow ourselves to feel what they feel, understanding their suffering at an emotional level. As we are empathetic and find ourselves caring for others, acts of altruism may arise.[6] This is the point at which empathy moves into the realm of compassion.

So while compassion may grow out of empathy, it is something quite different. Whereas empathy involves placing oneself metaphorically in the shoes of another ("I feel your pain"), compassion draws on the capacity to be present in the face of suffering and selflessly seek to eliminate it where it occurs ("I will work to relieve your pain").

The distinction between empathy and compassion is particularly relevant for those of us in caregiving professions such as teaching. In fact, this distinction highlights one of the most important reasons for teaching with compassion because it speaks to a commonly cited professional problem facing educators: burnout.

BURNOUT (OR COMPASSION FATIGUE)

Teacher burnout is a global phenomenon, and although there are many interpersonal and institutional explanations for it, one of the prevailing sentiments is that if we invest too much of ourselves in others, what sociologist Arlie Hochschild refers to as "emotional labor"—the constant managing and even suppressing of feelings in order to serve the needs of others[7]—then we will overcook our emotional and physical capacities and no longer be able to perform our duties.

Burnout among educators and other caregivers is often referred to as "compassion fatigue." But as Mattieu Ricard, the so-called happiest man in the world, points out, what is really happening in these instances is *empathy* fatigue, not compassion fatigue. Basing much of his ideas on Tania Singer's neuroscientific research, Ricard points out that the brain circuits that get activated for empathy are very different than those that get activated for compassion. People who undergo empathy training exclusively can actually experience increased negative feelings after a time. But when the same people then go through compassion training, not only do their negative feelings normalize, but they experience more positive feelings when exposed to bouts of suffering.

In other words, "by learning to transform empathy into compassion we not only better focus on the needs of others, we actually feel better overall."[8] Teaching with compassion is no guarantee that one will escape moments of feeling demoralized, overwhelmed, and exhausted from the demands of teaching; however, it does give us some tangible tools so that we can recognize, assuage, and even transform these feelings when we sense them creeping into our lives.

BENEFITS OF COMPASSION

The idea that we benefit when we act compassionately toward others makes perfect sense if we recognize compassion as an inherent human quality. By fully accepting the fact that compassion lives within each of us and by letting this natural inclination flourish, we come to realize the positives we gain. In his book *Rebel Buddha: On the Road to Freedom*, Dogchen Ponlop points out that acting compassionately toward others not only feeds their emotional well-being, but also nourishes our own well-being:

> Compassion is not a state that we manufacture in order to accomplish good works for someone else's benefit. It's part of our nature, our basic being, and when we connect with this nature, we're enriched and benefited at least as much as the person who is the object of our sympathy and concern. When we're genuinely engaged in a process of working with others, we're automatically working with ourselves as well.[9]

The Dalai Lama has expressed this sentiment even more succinctly: "If you want others to be happy, practice compassion; if you want to be happy, practice compassion."[10]

The benefits we gain from acting compassionately toward others extend beyond our own happiness. By consciously working to relieve the pain and suffering of others, we also cultivate the confidence to act more courageously: "Once both heart and mind are opened and joined and working together, we become more bold and daring."[11] This important point broadens the scope of this book. Teaching with compassion is not only about being kind to others nor is it solely about being kind to ourselves. It is also about entering the classroom with more verve, more fearlessness, and more adventure.

Teaching with compassion pulls us away from teaching in a manner that may feel stale, stagnant, robotic, and hackneyed, and moves us toward teaching with a sense of creativity, flexibility, ingenuity, and excitement. In effect, we may come to teaching with compassion because of an expressed desire to better the lives of students; however, we may be surprised by how much it also betters our lives as teachers.

WHAT IS TEACHING WITH COMPASSION?

Most of the commentaries about incorporating compassion into our lives as educators are found in the growing collection of books on mindfulness. Some recent books, such as *Pedagogies of Kindness and Respect*[12] and *Teaching with Tenderness*,[13] fall more within the tradition of Nel Noddings classic work on care in schools.[14] In the past five years or so, there has also been an exciting proliferation of books on teaching and learning with mindfulness.[15] These books provide wonderful insight and guidance for a more humanistic education, and they often introduce readers to a critical component of the humanist framework: compassion. *Teaching with Compassion* builds on this growing body of work by developing a specific overview and framework for a pedagogy of kindness, care, and concern.

There is no singular way to teach with compassion. Just as acts of compassion may take various forms depending on the circumstances and the individuals involved, so too teaching with compassion is somewhat situationally dependent. Compassion arises in situations when the heart is open and connected. However, there is no shame in not being able to respond to everyone with a full and open heart. Compassion is not something we expect, force, or shame others into, nor do we want to force our preconceived notions of compassion onto others.

Although we can acknowledge that treating others with dignity, care, and respect is our baseline orientation, we should bear in mind that the manner through which educators may exhibit compassion is not meant to be fixed or strictly prescribed. Teaching is an unpredictable and ever-evolving process, so it is unrealistic to think that there is a one-size-fits-all formula for how to teach with compassion in every situation. As such, the suggestions presented in this book are not intended to be the definitive account of what it means to teach with compassion. Instead, these points are offered as part of a developing and ongoing dialogue.

Teaching with Compassion is organized around eight principles, each of which constitutes a chapter. Taken together, the eight principles compose the Teaching with Compassion Oath, akin to the Hippocratic Oath, which serves as a potent aid to both inspire compassionate teaching and remind teachers of the many compassion practices available to them.

From fifth-century Greece to modern times, physicians have continued to pledge their commitment to caring for others by taking the Hippocratic Oath, whose core principle is encapsulated by the phrase "Do No Harm." In much the same fashion, the overarching spirit behind *Teaching with Compassion* and the Teaching with Compassion Oath is to do no harm to students.

To help us realize our full potential as compassionate educators each chapter includes examples and exercises. This material can be considered collectively with other educators or examined privately during moments of self-introspection. The exercises can also be amended and adapted to make them more appropriate for various teaching situations and contexts. In working through these chapter exercises, it is important to allow for occasional moments of discomfort to arise. It is often these instances of uneasiness that serve as a vehicle for deeper reflection and growth.

We recognize that some of these eight principles may be more familiar or apparent than others, some may be easier to adopt and implement than others, and some may be more relevant or relatable than others. Whatever the case may be, we encourage readers to contemplate these eight principles and then engage in discussion about them with others.

TEACHING WITH COMPASSION OATH

The emotional, social, and intellectual well-being of students is my main priority and my actions as an educator shall reflect this goal. As such, I vow to follow, to the best of my ability and judgment, these principles:

1. *Practice Beginner's Mind.* I see myself as unfinished so that I can learn from and honor what students bring to the classroom.
2. *Follow the Golden Rule.* Imagining myself as a student in the classroom, I treat students with dignity and respect and I nourish their genuine desire to learn.
3. *Learn from Adversity.* I try to understand difficult situations so that I may connect with and respond to pain and suffering within myself and students.
4. *Leave My Ego at the Door.* Through humility and a sense of vulnerability, I bring an open and welcoming heart to my teaching.
5. *Focus on Classroom Chemistry.* I aim to cultivate a cohesive community of learners in order to foster a humanizing educational experience.
6. *Listen with Intention.* I listen deeply, wholly, and actively to students by taking in their words, gestures, and silence.
7. *Hold Space.* Knowing that students experience stress and uncertainty, I provide opportunities for feeling, reflection, and expression.
8. *Teach like the Sun.* Wanting students to reach their full potential, I radiate warmth across the entire classroom and offer all students my attention.

Using real-life examples and excerpts from other authors and educators, each chapter is designed to illustrate what it means to be compassionate educators. Each chapter also concludes with a series of questions for further reflection that are designed to help readers further apply these principles to their own experiences as educators.

By way of concluding, we offer the following caveat and confession.

First, the caveat: The points we make in this book are not easily achievable. This book, and the Teaching with Compassion Oath, should not be approached as a checklist of goals. The aim is not to master each principle and then move on to the next point. Teaching with compassion is a lifelong journey. And the process, not the endpoint, is the focus of our book.

None of us will ever be able to declare with confidence and sincerity that we live by all of the principles of this oath in all moments of our teaching lives. That ideal is just not feasible. However, we can say that we are cognizant of these points and that we try to live by them. When we fail to live up to some of these ideals, and failure is inevitable, then we acknowledge our shortcomings and work to address them. Teaching with compassion does not mean that we are perfect or even perfectly compassionate. It means that we place our best intentions on bringing loving presence and a desire to understand and alleviate suffering to whatever arises in the moment.

Further, as we're working to cultivate compassion within ourselves as teachers and as living beings, we might consider holding it lightly and realizing that compassion is something that develops within us, organically and unforced. We may create conditions for compassionate responses, but if we promote rigid ideas of what compassion should look like, we may find ourselves sorely disappointed in others and find that true compassion eludes us.

Finally, just as we may hold off expectations that others express compassion in certain ways, so too can we release our expectations after we ourselves have expressed compassion. Teaching with compassion is its own reward. We do not need any accolades, awards, recognition, or special notoriety. Being able to teach with an unguarded and open heart is a great gift.

And now, the confession: It is often said that we teach best what we need to learn most. If this is true, what does it suggest about writing a book on how to teach with compassion? To us, admittedly, it means we are partially writing this book because we realize our own need to become more adept at teaching with compassion. We are in no way approaching this book from a perch of proficiency. We are not presuming to have unlocked the secrets, or our hearts, to teaching with love, kindness, respect, and dignity for all who we encounter. Indeed, just the opposite is true: we need as much guidance on these matters as any other educator.

Although we have certainly given thought to many of the issues we raise in these pages, thinking about them does not always translate into acting upon them. For us, working on this book was and continues to be a vehicle to challenge and critique ourselves, to reflect and respond to our work as educators, and to propose and practice strategies for teaching with compassion. We hope it serves the same purposes for you.

Chapter One

Practice Beginner's Mind

I see myself as unfinished so that I can learn from and honor what students bring to the classroom.

There is a well-known parable about a professor who pays a visit to a Zen master in hopes of gaining enlightenment. Within minutes of being welcomed, the professor, a renowned expert in his field, launches into a lengthy description of his accomplishments, the texts he has studied, and all of the books he has written.

The Zen master sits quietly and listens.

After much time passes, the master rises to make tea. When it is ready, he pours it into the professor's cup. But when the cup is full he keeps pouring. Soon, the tea is overflowing and spilling onto the floor. When the professor finally becomes aware of this he shouts, "Stop, stop! The cup is already full! There is no room left for any more tea." At this point, the master stops pouring and says to the professor: "You are like this cup of tea. You are so full of your own knowledge and expertise that there is no room for anything else. I can't teach you about Zen unless you first empty your cup."

Emptying our cup and practicing beginner's mind is one of the basic components of teaching with compassion. When we practice beginner's mind we start each school day with an empty cup, in much the same way we hope our students start each day, with a genuine openness to what is new and different. We are excited about *learning* new ideas and concepts, *discovering* things we did not know existed, *noticing* things for the very first time, *seeing* things from a different perspective, *realizing* things we may have ignored, and *appreciating* things we have long taken for granted.

The beginner's mind incorporates the best virtues of a child-like mind—one that is not yet set in its ways but is primed for exploration and wonder; one that is not yet indoctrinated into the "right" way of thinking but is willing to entertain and consider various explanations; and one that does not have any sense of grand accomplishments but is always interested in understanding more. Shunryu Suzuki, a Zen monk who helped popularize Buddhism in the West and is credited with coining the term *beginner's mind*, famously expressed, "In the beginner's mind there are many possibilities, but in the expert's mind there are few."[1]

Admittedly, practicing beginner's mind may not come easy for many of us and it may even seem counterintuitive. We have gone through years of specialized training, we have taught hundreds if not thousands of students the same concepts and ideas, and we may have written countless lesson plans, curriculum guides, articles, and even books. We refer to ourselves and are referred to by others as specialists or experts in our field. We may even be asked to speak about our area of expertise at faculty meetings, conferences, and workshops.

Indeed, our entire identity may be centered on our deep knowledge and understanding of a particular focus of our discipline: *I am a language arts specialist . . . a science teacher . . . a medieval historian . . . a scholar of Shakespeare*. After so many years of identifying and being identified as an expert, how could we possibly empty our cup and practice beginner's mind?

To make matters worse, there are numerous institutional forces that make practicing beginner's mind seem utterly unfathomable. There is much pressure on educators at every level to ensure students master specific skill sets, absorb a specified body of knowledge, and reach numerous preset outcomes. With assessments of students' learning driving the educational agenda from kindergarten all the way through college, trying to come to the classroom with an empty cup may seem foolish or even impossible. But by entering the classroom with genuine excitement to learn from students, we demonstrate that we welcome their contributions, we value what they have to offer, and we appreciate their unique insights and perspectives.

Practicing beginner's mind enlightens the lives of educators, but more importantly, it affirms the lives of students. When we empty our cups and willingly let them be filled with information from the class, we model a more collaborative and humanistic way of teaching and learning. We also let students see that despite the alienating and overbearing focus on standardized tests and grade point averages, there is another way for all of us to learn and grow in the classroom.

EXERCISE: WHAT DO YOU WANT TO LEARN?

The following exercise can be done with any grade level and is designed to help both students and teachers practice beginner's mind. The exercise also demonstrates how affirming it is for students to realize not only that they can teach their teacher but also that they can teach the teacher something he or she genuinely wants to learn.

The exercise is usually done in two consecutive class sessions but it can be modified easily to be completed in one session if that is all time allows.

Class Session 1

Ask students to take out a piece of paper and write at the top *What do I want to learn?* Going every other line, have them make a numbered list of ten things they want to learn. Some students might have a hard time thinking of ten things. It might be necessary to provide examples, perhaps from your own list or lists from other classes.

When everyone is finished, give students the opportunity to review each of their classmate's lists and add their names next to the things they also want to learn. Depending on class size, age, and setup of the classroom, this review can be structured in different ways:

1. Students can simply pass their lists to their neighbor on the right, review the list, write their names next to any of the things they also want to learn, and pass the list again to the right until all lists have been reviewed by all students. When everyone has had a chance to review everyone's paper, or as many papers as time and class size allows, students get their original papers back. They can then look to see how many people in the class, including the teacher, also want to learn some of the same things that they would like to learn.

2. Another approach, one that works well with younger students and gives them an opportunity to get out of their seats, is to have students post their responses around the classroom on large poster-sized sheets. You could write these out yourself after reviewing their lists and leave off names if you have concerns about protecting students from other students' comments. (Such an approach would require extending this into two separate sessions.) Students could walk around the room and place large check marks next to what they want to learn. This results in a visual representation of students' passions, intellectual curiosity, and desire to learn for all to see.

Class Session 2

For step 2 of the exercise, which can be done in another class session, students can use the back of the same sheet of paper or take out a new piece if necessary. At the top of the paper everyone writes the question *What can you teach us?* Once again, everyone will write down ten things that they can teach others. Responses need not be related to the course material but can encompass everyday lessons such as riding a bicycle, speaking a language, even tying one's shoes.

When everyone is finished, papers are passed around and everyone writes their name next to the answers that they would like to learn. So, for example, if someone writes down that they can teach someone how to speak Spanish and that's something that you want to learn then you would write your name next to that answer. After the papers have been passed around, everyone gets their original responses back.

As in the first stage of the exercise, everyone will see how many people in the class would like to learn some of the things that they can teach. Students are quick to realize that there are many things they really want to learn just as there are things that they can teach that are in high demand from others, including the teacher. Note, this second part of the exercise can be structured for younger children using the poster approach described earlier. And you can decide whether to share students' names.

For elementary or multisubject classrooms there are numerous opportunities for teachers to formally build on this exercise, crafting assignments where students have the opportunity to teach the class or creating special projects that bring students together with similar or different skills and interests.

But this exercise also offers opportunities for teachers at all levels to get to know students and use that knowledge to communicate to students that you are listening and valuing their contributions. For example, having learned that a student can teach Mandarin or blues guitar, you might want to consult that student and draw on her or his knowledge either as part of a class discussion or in a casual conversation. Perhaps you are teaching English and a grammar lesson may spark a discussion of how syntax is handled in other languages, such as Mandarin. Or a discussion of poetry might raise a question regarding blues lyrics or songwriters. The idea here isn't to put students on the spot, something it is always important to be sensitive to, but to let yourself and your classroom be empty enough to invite such contributions. Create a vacuum and students can fill it.

REKINDLING THE FLAME
OF INTELLECTUAL CURIOSITY

Sometimes when we do this exercise it is difficult for students to complete their two lists. Some of them cannot readily identify ten things they want to learn and others have difficulty identifying things they feel confident in teaching to others. For those insights alone, this exercise is an important one. If students are unable to articulate what it is they want to learn, much less what they are able to teach, it may be a sign that there is work to be done to rekindle their intellectual curiosity and the confidence they have in themselves as learners.

Most students entered formal schooling with an insatiable desire to take in new knowledge. They were sponges of information, constantly asking questions such as "Why does this happen?" "How is this possible?" "Where is so and so?" and "When does this occur?" Something transpired along the way during their formal schooling that smothered their natural curiosity and replaced it with intellectual indifference.

Erik Erikson, one of the leading psychoanalysts of the twentieth century, referred to this "mutilation of a child's spirit" as "the most deadly of all possible sins."[2] As educators committed to teaching with compassion, our primary goal is to be cognizant of this damage so that we can work to reignite the students' interest in learning.

One of the first steps to rekindling intellectual curiosity is ensuring that our own curiosity is burning brightly. Brazilian educator Paulo Freire has pointed out that if we do not exhibit the same "restless questioning" that young students exhibit, if we do not see ourselves as unfinished and embrace beginner's mind, then we will be unsuccessful in helping students realize their full human potential: "As a teacher, I cannot help the student to overcome their ignorance if I am not engaged permanently in trying to overcome my own."[3]

By modeling beginner's mind in an open and encouraging way for students, we encourage them to reawaken the love of learning that is still flickering somewhere inside of them—no matter how deeply buried it may be. In this sense, beginner's mind and intellectual curiosity become the keys that unlock the students' humanness. But they are particularly useful in helping us to unlock our *own* humanness, or compassion, as educators. Curiosity gives us the inclination to step outside our comfort zone, to awaken our senses to the lives, patterns, and processes of others.

Indeed, as Freire notes, the "movement toward the revelation of something hidden" is "an integral part of the phenomenon of being alive."[4] Without beginner's mind, without curiosity, we are content to stay in our secluded, taken-for-granted worlds and we fail to see that our way of being is just one variation on many themes. But the more we are truly receptive to learning from others, particularly students, and we recognize our interdependence with them, the more we free ourselves to teach with compassion.

HUMILITY AS A PATH TO TEACHING HUMANELY

One of our favorite stories of a teacher practicing beginner's mind, approaching her students from a position of humility and openness, comes from an elementary school teacher who recounted how she learned the secret to solving Rubik's Cube from an enthusiastic group of fourth graders. This teacher remembered playing with the Rubik's Cube when she was younger but was never able to crack the code. These students, with the help of the Internet, were not only able to do something that their teacher was unable to master; more importantly, they were able to proudly teach her how to do something that she always wanted to learn.

This story may seem trivial, but to the fourth-grade students who suddenly found themselves in the position of being teachers it was anything but trivial. In this relatively brief encounter with their teacher, a world of possibilities was open to them. They were given a platform, a voice, and a willing audience, or student, to whom they could share their knowledge. No matter what else may have been going on in their lives, inside or outside of school, that positive encounter with their teacher was a boost to their spirits, their confidence, and their sense of importance.

It should be obvious that beginner's mind and humility are mutually reinforcing. As educator and philosopher Paulo Freire asks, "how can we respect the curiosity of students if we are lacking genuine humility?"[5]

FREEING OURSELVES OF ASSUMPTIONS

Consider the following story:

> A Navajo student freezes as she enters her second-grade classroom. It is the first day of school and she stands motionless and will not talk. The teacher assumes that she just has a case of the first-day jitters and will get over it. The teacher is kind and encouraging: "I remember what it was like for me on the first day of second grade. I felt scared, too," he shares. Yet the student will not walk into the classroom. The teacher cannot seem to make any headway with the girl and eventually contacts the principal.
>
> The student gets even more reticent and noncommunicative with the principal. The principal loses patience and demands that the student go to her class.

She complies and yet remains withdrawn and unfriendly. A few weeks pass and parent-teacher night arrives. The girl's father walks into the classroom and freezes, just like his daughter did on the first day of school. However, he can articulate the problem in a way that his daughter could not: "You have a snake in your room. In the Navajo way snakes are taboo. Even crossing a snake's path is dangerous."

This story is a powerful reminder that we do not know what goes on in the lives of students unless we are actively committed to learning about them. Unless we make it our business to find out, we do not know how their experiences and cultural lenses shape who they are and how they come to view the world, including their view of school. And we will certainly not know their fears, insecurities, anxieties, worries, pain, and suffering unless we are willing to bear witness to what they are willing to share with us.

How often do we think we know what type of student we are dealing with without even speaking a word with them? We may see how they are dressed, how they walk into a room, where and how they sit in their chair, and we automatically label them as this or that type of student. We may also form an opinion of them by relying on stereotypes, gossip from other teachers, experiences with the students' friends, or the reputation of their siblings who preceded them. But by walking into the classroom each day with beginner's mind and humility, we signal to students that we are not only open to learning *from* them but also interested in learning *about* them.

We are telling them plainly and directly that our relationship with them is starting fresh, with a blank slate that hasn't been written on with hearsay, rumors, or stereotypes, and thus that we are open to knowing them wholly and authentically.

This clear and friendly invitation to students to share with us who they are is one of the first steps in establishing the rapport that makes teaching with compassion possible. If students do not sense that we are interested in learning about them, then it is highly unlikely that they will open up to us in any meaningful ways. In her work with some of the most challenging students in New York City schools, Dana Ashley, director of the Positive Learning Collaborative, has found that the most effective teachers are the ones that take the time to build positive relationships with students.[6]

But in extending this invitation, we must recognize that not all students will readily accept our overture. For some, the wounds they may have endured from what educator Mary Rose O'Reilley has called "academic brutalization" are too deep to easily forget.[7] These students may be leery, suspicious, and distrustful of teachers. We may have to be explicit about our intentions and patient with our expectations.

Just because we invite students with open arms does not mean that they will waltz right in and join us. It may take days, months, or even years to gain their trust. But as with many of the themes that we are discussing here, opening our hearts and minds to students is the goal. Knowing that there will always be some students who are tentative about or even outright reject our invitation should only make us more resolute in finding ways to reach out and connect.

A BALM FOR STRESSED AND BUSY STUDENTS

When we talk with students and colleagues about practicing beginner's mind, we often get asked how we can come to see ourselves as empty when our lives are so full.[8] Indeed, our cups are overflowing with digital media, news, responsibilities, goals, deadlines, and worries. Addicted to this busyness, neither we nor our students seem to have the time or even the inclination to empty our cups.

In fact, many of us shun downtime and look condescendingly on those who claim to have nothing to do. We prefer to have our schedules packed to the brim so we can run, sometimes literally, from one obligation to the next. Think about it: when was the last time you asked another teacher how they are doing and they *didn't* reply, "Busy," "Overwhelmed," or "Just trying to stay afloat"? We hear these responses all of the time, almost as if they are a badge of honor.

And it is not just our colleagues who feel this way. Students also feel particularly harried by time pressures. Between studying, extracurricular activities, volunteering, working, socializing, and a host of other responsibilities and obligations, many students today feel maxed out. We are often amazed and somewhat startled when we hear from undergraduates about how overwhelmed they feel with all that they have to get done in a day. For many of them, pulling all-nighters is a regular part of their weekly routine. They pack their schedules with extracurricular activities, community service, internships, test prep courses, and other undertakings so that they can stand out in the eyes of admissions counselors and job recruiters. The "overscheduled" or "pressured" student is evident across all grade levels.[9]

Students hope that the ends will justify their busy means; however, as they go through this harried existence they feel stressed out, overwhelmed, and uncertain. The more they do, the more frazzled they become, but if they do less they risk becoming even more anxious because they may feel as if they are not measuring up. Their daily existence becomes a series of hoops that they jump through with the hope that one day they will be able to grab the elusive golden ring.

This existence is draining, stressful, and taxing. The physical and emotional toll that such stress produces affects students' sleeping and eating patterns, their ability to focus and concentrate, and their daily disposition and outlook. This cult of busyness compromises students' abilities to grow emotionally, to develop intellectually, and to thrive socially. With their schedules and calendars so full, there are fewer possibilities for exploring one's interests, fewer opportunities for entertaining one's curiosities, and fewer occasions for learning something that is not part of the standard curriculum. Given the extent to which they feel so overextended, is it any wonder that more students today are experiencing symptoms of anxiety and depression than ever before?[10]

As teachers we can choose to jump on this bandwagon of busyness, this chase after expertise and credentials, or we can help students see there are alternatives. When we practice beginner's mind, model it to the students, and show them how they too can empty their cups, we provide them with a compassionate antidote to their overextended, hectic, and stressed-out lives. In making a commitment to teach with compassion, we ensure that not only are we aware of this growing trend but that we will do everything we can to keep this toxic reality out of our teaching and out of the classroom. We can do this by finding ways to help students empty their cups, carve out a few moments to de-stress and recharge. Here are two versions of a short, five-minute exercise that we have found useful.

❦

EXERCISE: EMPTY YOUR CUP

Version 1: At the beginning of class, take the first five minutes to go around the room and have everyone say, in quick succession, what it is they would like to empty from their cups. Maybe it is an upcoming test they are stressing over, a relationship issue, a crappy job, an annoying sibling, or something else that is causing worry and anxiety. The point is to allow each student to symbolically empty their cup and publicly acknowledge what is weighing on their mind. You can continue going around the room allowing students to further empty their cups until the five minutes are up.

Version 2: Give everyone a few scraps of paper and ask them to write one response on each piece of paper of what they would like to empty from their cup. You can then have someone move around the room with a garbage can and each student can empty their cup by throwing away their responses.

Alternatively, you can set the garbage can in the middle of the room and have students toss their responses into the can.

The Empty Your Cup exercise is a fun way to acknowledge the stressors that students are experiencing. And because it only takes about five minutes, it is well suited for even those of us who have the strictest and most time-dependent curriculum to follow. This exercise tells students that we understand some of what they are experiencing and that we want to help them relieve some of the busyness-related stress that they are experiencing. The Empty Your Cup exercise is in no way meant to be a panacea to the students' stress and worry. Nevertheless, finding a mere five minutes in our day to recognize and work through some the students' stress and worry sends an important and heartfelt message.

CONCLUDING THOUGHTS

Practicing beginner's mind is the first principle of the Teaching with Compassion Oath because in many ways it is the gateway to teaching with compassion. Arguably, it is a necessary mind-set from which the seven other principles follow. After all, how can we learn from and honor what students bring to the classroom if we do not see ourselves as unfinished? How do we give voice to and respect students if we are not willing to enter the classroom with a sense of humility and modesty? And how can we demonstrate boundless compassion for students if our minds (or cups) are so full and occupied? Practicing beginner's mind frees us from these limiting obscurations and allows us to enter the classroom with the type of open mind that is necessary for an open heart.

In his famous explanation of the beginner's mind, Shunryu Suzuki uses the word *possibilities* to capture the unlimited opportunities for growth and development. Another word we may consider is *promise*. Like possibilities, promise also connotes infinite potential for becoming more fully human. But promise also has two other interpretations that reflect the core of teaching with compassion.

First, there is the students' promise. When we practice beginner's mind it is not only our promise for growth and development that is unleashed; the students' promise for growth, development, and becoming more fully human is also liberated.

This point gets to the second interpretation of promise: a vow or an assurance that we implicitly, or explicitly, make to students to treat them with kindness, generosity, concern, and respect. Teaching with compassion is a process or mind-set that we engage in as educators with the recognition that students are the endpoints of our actions.

We make the conscious effort to teach with compassion, and it is indeed an effort, because we are aware of the importance of our actions as educators. When we walk into the classroom with beginner's mind, and we make this known to students through our words, actions, and even the layout of the classroom, we signal to students that we are there *for* them and *with* them. We are making a promise to them that in this classroom, the possibilities are indeed endless.

QUESTIONS FOR FURTHER REFLECTION

1. Can you think of an instance when you were like the professor in the Zen tale at the beginning of this chapter? What exactly did you feel you knew so much about? Did you know at the time that your cup was overflowing, or was it only in retrospect that you realized it?
2. What do you think are the biggest impediments to having the beginner's mind? Are they personal, social, or institutional?
3. You may have heard the idea that oftentimes the best teachers come from the most unlikely and unexpected sources. Can you recollect some people from your life who were "unlikely teachers"? What things did they teach you?
4. Are there collective efforts at the department, school, or district level that could be taken to help educators learn from and about students? What might some of these initiatives look like? Could they be incorporated into the curriculum or would they be extracurricular?
5. In what ways do teachers knowingly and unknowingly contribute to students feeling busy and overextended? Other than the Empty Your Cup exercise, which is largely symbolic, are there changes in your teaching that can be feasibly implemented that might help students feel less caught up in the busy trap?

Chapter Two

Follow the Golden Rule

Imagining myself as a student in the classroom, I treat students with dignity and respect and I nourish their genuine desire to learn.

The Golden Rule has long been one of the major pillars of compassion and it is easy to see why. Implicit in the Golden Rule is imagining yourself in the position of the other. Karen Armstrong explains the connection in this passage from her *Twelve Steps to a Compassionate Life*:

> So "compassion" means "to endure [something] with another person," to put ourselves in somebody else's shoes, to feel her pain as though it were my own, and to enter generously into his point of view. That is why compassion is aptly summed up in the Golden Rule, which asks us to look into our own hearts, discover what gives us pain, and then refuse, under any circumstances whatsoever, to inflict that pain on anybody else. Compassion can be defined, therefore, as an attitude of principled, consistent, altruism.[1]

The idea of treating people the way you would like to be treated is such a simple and basic idea. It is no wonder that many of us learn this lesson when we are children. It makes good sense that if you want to be treated with dignity and respect, then you will treat other people the same way. If you prefer it when people interact with you in a friendly, responsive, and welcoming manner, then you will likely strive to exude those same qualities. And if you appreciate feeling care, concern, and compassion from others then the Golden

Rule teaches us that you will interact with others through expressions of care, concern, and compassion.

Yet, we know all too well that we do not always treat others with the same respect, patience, friendliness, and concern that we might expect to receive from them, especially when it comes to how we make the thousands of decisions we are asked to make every day as teachers. In their short meditation, *On Kindness*, psychoanalyst and essayist Adam Phillips and historian Barbara Taylor offer this insightful bit of commentary: "We are never as kind as we want to be, but nothing outrages us more than people being unkind to us. There is nothing we feel more consistently deprived of than kindness; the unkindness of others has become our contemporary complaint. Kindness consistently preoccupies us, and yet most of us are unable to live a life guided by it."[2]

As we dive into the work of creating lessons, structuring our classrooms, crafting assignments, and setting expectations for students, how often do we let our own experience as students inform our choices? It probably does not take a stretch of one's imagination to identify something off-putting that was done to us when we were students that we now find ourselves repeating as teachers. Maybe it was a particular type of assignment, a manner of responding to students in class, or an uninspiring teaching methodology. Whatever the case, it is likely that there are pedagogical practices that made learning less than pleasurable for us as students, practices that we may even have complained of bitterly, that we are now, maybe innocently and unwittingly, replicating as educators.

Assuming that none of us are born great or horrible teachers, it follows that we learn to be educators from our past experiences and our professional socialization. Of course, K–12 teachers get the benefit of explicit pedagogical instruction and practice, while those in postsecondary education are often left to fend for themselves with little or no formal training in pedagogy and may be unaware of the latest research on high-impact educational practices. Still, as much as this training may give K–12 teachers an edge when it comes to challenging and rethinking their early classroom experiences, the reality is that it is all too easy to fall back on deeply rooted, formative experiences, rationalizing that it worked for us so why not for our students.

In *Pedagogy of the Oppressed*, Paulo Freire warns that when those who were in subjugated or subservient positions gain some degree of power, they must actively resist the inclination to assert their dominance over others: "The oppressed must not, in seeking to regain their humanity (which is a way to create it), become in turn oppressors."[3] In our time as students, there may have been moments where we felt disrespected, ignored, misunderstood, treated unfairly, and maybe even oppressed by a teacher. It is useful to remember such instances as they can serve an important function in ensuring that we do not replicate such behaviors, and essentially negate the Golden Rule, in our role as teachers.

PUTTING THE GOLDEN RULE INTO ACTION

The good news is that these negative experiences provide an excellent basis for seriously applying the Golden Rule in the classroom. As sociologist Lory Dance points out in the edited collection *Everyday Antiracism: Getting Real about Race in Schools*, reflecting back on situations when we were wronged can help us open our hearts fully to students:

> If we want to prompt young people never to treat others as inferior, we must first reflect upon moments when our own humanity was insulted, bruised, battered, or robbed, or when we may have insulted, bruised, battered or robbed the humanity of another person. We can consider how we ourselves did or did not heal from such events, and prepare to offer better healing experiences to our students.[4]

Dance refers to the experience of having been "insulted, bruised, battered, or robbed" of humanity. Of course, this is extreme and the purpose here is not to suggest that teachers may be revisiting such experiences on students. But Dance's point about the importance of reflecting on wrongs, on when we may have suffered from infractions against the Golden Rule, still applies to many less extreme but difficult experiences. The following exercise, which can be done individually or in a group setting, is a first step in the process of reflection.

EXERCISE: WHAT GOES AROUND
DOES NOT COME AROUND

Think back to when you were a student and were treated unfairly or unkindly by a teacher, when your concerns were ignored or not even listened to, your experiences discounted, your fears dismissed as if they didn't matter, or maybe your knowledge or skills not just underappreciated but completely unrecognized. In short, think of a time when you felt you were not treated with respect and dignity. If you cannot recall a specific example from your own experience, then you can use an example you observed either during your own schooling or in your professional life as a teacher. This could be a single incident or a pattern of behavior. Once you have an example in mind take some time to reflect on and write about the *who, what, why,* and *how* of this experience:

- *Who?* Who were the actors involved? Identify the characteristics of these actors (position, age, year in school, gender, race, etc.). Who else witnessed this behavior or incident? Who set the tone of the interactions?
- *What?* What was said or done? What response did this elicit from others? What was the fallout?
- *Why?* Why was this experience so upsetting to you? Why has it stayed with you in your memory? Why do you think the actors acted the way they did in this situation?
- *How?* How might the actors have acted differently? How would you act differently if you were in this situation—particularly if you were in a position of power? How might you explain to those involved that there are alternative forms of reacting and responding?

As you imagine alternatives, you will come upon some situations that are straightforward and call for pretty obvious and doable behavior changes.

> Yes, I remember how I hated being teased by my English teacher in front of the whole class because I wrote about my dog every chance I got. I certainly wouldn't want to do the same to my students.
>   *Or*
> It was unfair that my fifth-grade teacher refused to listen when I tried to explain why I couldn't bring my project in on time, even though it was because my mother had been rushed to the emergency room the night before. Perhaps I need to listen to and do a better job of hearing students out.

But others aren't so clear cut. For example, there may be many educational practices we detested when we were students whose value we might appreciate now. Indeed, we realize that part of our job is to challenge students to go beyond their comfort zones so that they develop socially, emotionally, and intellectually. To follow the Golden Rule does not mean that we omit things from our teaching practices just because they were or still are uncomfortable or unappealing. Instead, we want to tap into these memories and strong aversions, to use them as both guidance and inspiration in helping students overcome their own fears and discomforts.

Consider the following example: A middle-school teacher was having her students do an oral presentation on one of the books they read during their summer reading program. For a number of students in the class this was an anxiety-producing assignment. It was the beginning of the school year, the students were in their first year in this middle school, and some had no experience presenting in front of the class.

When students objected and expressed their obvious discomfort, the teacher could have responded in any number of ways. She could have taken a "tough love" approach, telling students, "Sorry, that's part of being a middle school student. It's just something you have to do." Or, in an effort to acknowledge students' concerns and respond with empathy, she could have offered some encouragement and reassurance, "You will all do great. Everyone is scared at first, but most students like it in the end. Don't worry about it." Or she could do what this teacher did.

First, she allowed herself to reflect on the nature of her own shaky experiences as a middle schooler. This teacher had moved around quite a bit as a child and it always took her some time to find her comfort zone in her new schools. She was also terrified of public speaking. As a young child she had a pronounced lisp and was often teased about it. Although the lisp was eventually corrected through speech therapy, the memories of the stigma had a lasting effect, especially when she had to do public speaking.

Using her understanding of her own experience, this teacher employed a number of strategies to try to mitigate the students' anxiety. She presented them with a template on which to base their presentation; she set aside time for them to practice their presentations in small groups; and she introduced them to breathing exercises intended to calm their nerves.

Maybe most importantly, she not only shared her own middle school experiences as being fearful of this exact type of assignment; she also had two students from the previous year come to the class and briefly share similar experiences of going from panicky to poised. In effect, she tried to take the sort of proactive steps of teaching with compassion that she wished her teachers had done for her many years ago.

By seriously respecting and honoring students' feelings, by taking their dignity and humanity into account, the teacher ended up crafting a more effective, engaging, and even challenging learning experience than if she had asked students to "just do it" without complaint. This is what can result when we recognize the humanity of every student with whom we come into contact by treating them with the same integrity and decency that we expect from others. In short, teaching by the Golden Rule can be summed up in two words: respect and dignity.

RESPECT: THE FOURTH R

School days, school days, dear old golden rule days
Readin' and 'ritin' and 'rithmetic
Taught to the tune of the hick'ry stick

It's not altogether surprising that this popular 1907 song by Will Cobb and Gus Edwards invokes the Golden Rule. We have all heard about the three Rs of schooling. Maybe it's time to add a fourth R to this list: respect.

Respect is paramount for a successful teaching and learning environment; without it, we cannot truly nourish students' genuine desire to learn. When we talk about respect, we usually refer to the term in relation to people—we should respect others and respect ourselves.

When we teach with compassion, we strive to establish genuine and oftentimes deep connections with students. While this may be a challenge to those of us who teach large lectures or high school teachers who see as many as eighty or one hundred students passing through their rooms each day, as much as possible we need to find ways to view each student as a unique and distinct individual.

To follow the Golden Rule in our teaching means making the conscious effort to avoid labels and stereotypes, such as *lazy*, *not serious*, and *checked out*, or even seemingly positive labels such as *good student* or *A student*—no matter how apt they may seem. Instead, we work to take time to appreciate the distinctive qualities that make students who they are. Treating others with respect is a form of interpersonal mindfulness: we pay attention to the other, honoring their state of being, and valuing what they bring to the situation.

Students often gravitate toward those educators who show an interest in them and treat them with care and concern. Which educators did you feel connected to or appreciated by when you were a student? And what educators did you seek out for advice, encouragement, or a favor? Most likely, it was those educators who treated you with respect, just as you are a source of support for your students when you treat them similarly.

Unfortunately, the landscape of education continually presents challenges to us to achieve these goals. For instance, we may be forced to spend too much time on assessment measures and bureaucratic minutia at the expense of cultivating curiosity, creativity, and interpersonal connections. We may also lack the institutional support and the physical space to handle the overflow of students and their unique needs.

And then, of course, there is the not-so-hidden secret about our educational institutions: many of them are in various states of disrepair. Whether it's classrooms with old and decrepit desks, hallways with peeling paint and missing tiles, libraries with anemic and outdated book collections, or lunchrooms that serve double, triple, or even quadruple duty as gymnasiums, theaters, and detention halls, students and teachers at all educational levels often have to learn and teach in places that are less than ideal.

For those educators who must constantly endure the failing (or falling) infrastructure of their academic institutions, starting each day with passion and gusto can be challenging. It is easy to line up with our colleagues at the complaints department and air our list of grievances about the buildings and classrooms we must tolerate. Both of us teach at public institutions and we know all too well how years of budget cuts to education have left gaping holes, sometimes literally, in our schools. These grievances and concerns are all indeed real, and we should certainly advocate and organize for them to be addressed.

But despite all of the infrastructural problems we face and all of the valid gripes we may have about the conditions under which we teach, it is crucial to remember that for some students, school is a revered and valued refuge. School is a place that may offer a respite from a harsh and uncaring world. It may be a place that provides the only hot meal of the day or the only positive and healthy interactions. And it also may be a place that signifies the opportunities and prospects that early generations of relatives never had.

We may not all have the luxury of teaching in state-of-the-art facilities. However, that does not have to stop us from offering students a state-of-the-art educational experience. Just because the places we teach may be disrespected by those who hold the purse strings does not mean that we have to also treat the place or the people with disrespect and disdain. This point really gets at what it means to follow the Golden Rule: If we want to be teaching and learning in a place that is honored and respected, we need to treat that place in an honorable and respectful manner—even if it is disregarded and disparaged by others.

Instead of taking for granted all of the resources at our disposal, however imperfect they may be, let us acknowledge that we can still accomplish great things and make a big impact in students' lives with what we have. In short, just as we honor the sanctity of each student in the classroom, so too we should honor the sanctity of the spaces that make teaching and learning possible.

EXERCISE: RESPECT THROUGH ACROSTIC POETRY

The following exercise helps us think about the various ways that we may demonstrate respect in our daily teaching lives. If we want to teach in ways that we prefer to be taught and we want to nourish students' genuine desire to learn, then we need to be able to articulate what exactly that means.

This exercise uses acrostic poetry of the word *RESPECT*. It is a challenging but creative and engaging way to brainstorm about the multiple ways that we can act respectfully toward students. Because there are different ways to create an acrostic poem (the first, last, or other letters in the line can be used to spell out a particular word or phrase), this exercise has infinite possibilities. It can also be done multiple times, especially if you use a different acrostic parameter each time. We also suggest doing this exercise with colleagues or in a professional development workshop in order to hear the many different ways that other educators conceptualize respectful teaching.

Here is one example that builds words and phrases around the letters of RESPECT. Each sentence begins with the phrase "I will always try to" in order to acknowledge these affirmations as goals for compassionate teaching. When you do this exercise on your own, try playing around with your own guidelines and prompts.

I will always try to *R*espond thoughtfully and kindly to students.
I will always try to treat each student *E*qually.
I will always try to make the classroom a *S*afe space for students.
I will always try to remember that students are *P*eople, not test scores or reputations.
I will always try to be *E*ngaged and enthusiastic when working with students.
I will always try to nurture the innate *C*uriosity of each student.
I will always try to convey, through words and actions, that students can *T*rust me.

DIGNITY ABOVE ALL ELSE

"So here I stand, one girl among many. I speak not for myself, but so those without a voice can be heard. Those who have fought for their rights. Their right to live in peace. Their right to be treated with dignity. Their right to equality of opportunity. Their right to be educated."[5] These are the words of Nobel Prize laureate Malala Yousafzai in her address to the United Nations in July 2013. She gave this speech less than one year after the attempt on her life by the Taliban. Her message of equality, opportunity, and dignity for all females has resonated across the globe and has made her a world-renowned activist for education.

Malala's speech was about many things: intolerance, inequality, war, terrorism, violence, and ignorance. But at its core, her speech was about the

Golden Rule. She called upon world leaders, governments, developed nations, communities, and all people of the world to treat each other the way we all expect and deserve to be treated. Her speech echoed the first article of the "Universal Declaration of Human Rights," which focuses specifically on dignity: "All human beings are born free and equal in dignity and rights. They are endowed with reason and conscience and should act towards one another in a spirit of brotherhood."[6]

The emphasis on treating each other with dignity is central to teaching with compassion. But like some of the other concepts we discuss in this book, dignity is one of those ideas that we know to be a good thing but we may be less clear as to how it could inform our teaching. To better understand the connection between dignity and teaching with compassion we borrow from the late Jonathan Mann's writing about dignity and health.[7]

Mann was the former head of the World Health Organization's global AIDS program and staunch advocate for recognizing that human health and human rights must be understood together. He was particularly interested in dignity because he saw it as vitally important to the well-being of individuals and societies, and also because he saw it as increasingly under threat.

To address these two themes, Mann created a taxonomy of dignity violations so that people could better document when their dignity was violated. There are four points of the taxonomy: not being seen; humiliation; being subsumed into a group identity; and invasion of personal space. We focus specifically on the first two of these points.

Not Being Seen

The experience of not being seen typically occurs when individuals feel ignored, unacknowledged, disregarded, silenced, or irrelevant in the eyes of one to whom we look toward for validation. Even things as seemingly trivial as not making eye contact, not shaking hands, not welcoming people with a smile, or not recalling their names or anything about them may result in someone feeling slighted. Of course, we are all busy and overworked, but dedicating ourselves to ensuring that students feel seen by simply smiling or making eye contact is a first step. For Mann, our dignity is threatened when our humanity is unrecognized, when we are rendered invisible by others.

Another way teachers can make students feel unseen is a common practice we dub *teachersplaining*—a play on the current popular term *mansplaining*, an equally common practice whereby men take it upon themselves to explain things to women that they assume women don't know or that they need to know.

A well-known example of mansplaining occurs in writer Rebecca Solnit's viral essay "Men Explain Things to Me," where Solnit describes herself being detained by a man who insists on telling her all about a new book, oblivious to the fact that she was, in fact, the author of the book.[8] Mansplaining is a dignity violation because women's ideas, knowledge, insights, and potential contributions are ignored and discounted.

Of course, male educators should no doubt guard against and try to prevent instances of mansplaining to female students and colleagues. But avoiding instances of teachersplaining that may alienate and even violate the dignity of students may be a bigger challenge, because, after all, as teachers, it's our job to explain, isn't it? But maybe not.

Teachersplaining, to borrow the words of Paulo Freire, reflects the banking model of education where teachers see students as empty vessels to be filled with the content of the teacher's narration. In this model, the teacher talks and the students listen, the teacher is the subject and the students are mere objects, the teacher knows and the students don't know, the teacher makes choices and the students dutifully follow.[9]

When we ask undergraduate students if the teachersplaining paradigm characterizes their education (including their college classes), we get nearly universal agreement. Even thinking back to our own educations, it is undeniable that this was the dominant method of instruction. Teachersplaining, when allowed to dominate the classroom, can rob students of their intellectual dignity and their genuine desire to learn. As a result, it does not adequately lay the groundwork for lifelong learning. And it negates a basic premise of learning: creative exploration. As Freire points out, "To teach is to create the possibilities for the construction and production of knowledge rather than to be engaged simply in a game of transferring knowledge."[10]

All lecturing and fact giving is not teachersplaining. There are times when the best choice is to offer an answer, share an experience, provide necessary background knowledge. Like mansplaining, however, teachersplaining occurs when teachers make assumptions about students' knowledge and learning needs without first doing the work of gathering information about what students truly know and truly need. Taking this approach treats students with intellectual dignity and respect.

Humiliation

"You have A.J. in your class? That's too bad—she is the worst student in the entire fourth grade!"

We have probably all heard comments like this at one point or another. To be criticized harshly in the company of one's peers is no doubt a humiliating experience. But being subject to gossip and hearsay are equally troubling.

In fact, this type of dignity violation may be even more severe because the individual has no knowledge of the critique and subsequently no recourse to set the record straight.

Most of us know what it feels like to be embarrassed in front of others or to be subject to rumors and false stories. The wisdom we have gained from these hurtful experiences should help us resist subjecting students to these dignity violations.

But what are even more difficult to address are those times when we inadvertently or unintentionally humiliate students. Even the most altruistic and empathetic educators have experienced situations where students come away feeling ashamed and demeaned. Perhaps our comments or actions were interpreted differently than we intended; we assumed a level of familiarity or comfort with students that wasn't there; we failed to acknowledge their contribution to a discussion; or we had a moment where we were frustrated or lost patience and reacted in a way that was uncharacteristic.

One semester, when Peter was doing the Cultivating Beginner's Mind exercise (described in chapter 1) with his Introduction to Sociology class, he learned that one of his students came away humiliated because of a simple oversight on his part. The exercise asks students to make a list of different things they want to learn about. That day he had forgotten to mention that the list would be shared with the other students.

When the student, who had interpreted Peter's instructions to mean she was to write a list of things she wanted to improve upon, found out everyone would read her list, she was mortified. She went along with the exercise but sent an e-mail to Peter saying how humiliated and exposed she felt when she woke up the next morning.

Experiences like this are particularly instructive in helping us hone in on what it means to teach with compassion. As much as we may try to be fully attentive to students' feelings, perspectives, and even their interpretations, there is no way to fully safeguard against accidentally humiliating them. Knowing this, we need to redouble our efforts to create safe spaces and provide welcoming opportunities for students to convey to us when they may feel humiliated.

REPAIRING THE DAMAGE

But providing opportunities for students to communicate is just the first step. The second step is to repair the damage that we have unintentionally done. More than just apologizing we need to listen intently to the experiences of humiliation that students describe. We need to reflect back to them that they have been heard and their feelings acknowledged. And we need to assure them that we will do everything we can to avoid such violations from ever happening again. In these instances of inadvertent dignity violations, we owe it to the student to bear witness to their suffering and sit with our own discomfort in recognizing our fallibility.

Jonathan Mann reminds us that "injuries to dignity which occurred decades earlier continued to evoke powerful emotions."[11] This confirms much of our own anecdotal evidence gathered over many years in the classroom. We have witnessed the scars students carry from the negative experiences they have endured at some point or points in their schooling. It could be a recent experience or it could be something that happened to them in their primary school years. In any case, it is a necessary reminder to us as educators that our actions matter and can potentially have a lasting effect.

We conclude this chapter with a final exercise that we hope will further reinforce the importance of teaching by the Golden Rule. Part of the inspiration of this exercise comes from Jonathan Mann, who points to the importance of the Golden Rule as a model for our actions and behaviors: "For human rights can become meaningful only when people accord to others the dignity they assume for themselves."[12] The following exercise, which employs mantras, is intended to cement our adherence to the Golden Rule in our lives as educators.

എട്ടുൻ

EXERCISE: CREATING GOLDEN RULE MANTRAS

Zen-Buddhist teacher Thich Nhat Hanh, who has been using mantras—sacred words, sounds, or phrases—in his teachings for many years, offers a concise summary of both the potential and proper use of mantras:

> A mantra is a magic formula. Every time you pronounce a mantra you can transform the situation right away; you don't have to wait. Learn it so you can recite it when the time is appropriate. What makes the mantra effective is your mindfulness and concentration. If you aren't mindful and concentrated when you recite the mantra, it won't work. We are all capable of being mindful and concentrated.[13]

Some have used the Golden Rule as a mantra and it is easy to see why. It can be easily memorized and can be recited when we know we want to act in a more compassionate and forgiving manner.

> I vow to do unto others
> As I would have others do unto me

In thinking about how we may use the Golden Rule to teach with compassion we have found it useful to create mantras that convey our expectations for our own behaviors. Focusing on the overarching themes of respect and dignity, these mantras can remind us of what we value in the teaching and learning process and can help us focus our actions in accordance with these values.

Here are a few obvious ones to get you started:

> I strive to treat others with respect,
> just as I expect to be treated with respect.
>
> I affirm the dignity of others,
> just as I expect my dignity to be affirmed.
>
> I will not rely on stereotypes and labels,
> just as I do not want others to label and stereotype me.
>
> When students speak,
> I will check my understanding before I respond.

Try to think of your own mantras that reflect your approach to teaching and learning. If you are feeling really ambitious, try to create ten mantras that you can put up in your office, on your electronic device, or in your appointment book so that you are constantly reminded and encouraged to follow the Golden Rule. You may even want to use some of the Teaching with Compassion Oath points and turn these into mantras.

QUESTIONS FOR FURTHER REFLECTION

1. What do you do when the Golden Rule is not being reciprocated? In other words, how do you treat students with respect when they are being disrespectful to you? What strategies do you use to deal with this situation?
2. Instead of the Golden Rule, some people prefer what is often called the Platinum Rule: asking others how they want to be treated and then acting this way toward them. What are the pros and cons of following the Golden Rule versus the Platinum Rule?

3. Besides respect and dignity, what other themes might you focus on to teach by the Golden Rule?
4. Can you think of any teaching situations where it is not appropriate to follow the Golden Rule? What is it about these situations that might make the Golden Rule contextually inappropriate?
5. Do you think we need the Golden Rule now more than ever or is the Golden Rule always applicable and everlasting?

Chapter Three

Learn from Adversity

I try to understand difficult situations so that I may connect with and respond to pain and suffering within myself and students.

"Adversity will surface in every life. How we meet it makes the difference."

—Marvin J. Ashton

As we all know too well there is no shortage of adversity in our daily life as educators. We encounter underprepared and disruptive students. We have troubled students who have inflicted harm on themselves or others. We have conflicts with other colleagues or administrators. We get angry at students, angry at our colleagues and administrators, angry at government leaders, angry at parents, or just angry at the general state of affairs. We face racism, classism, and sexism, homophobia, and other -isms of intolerance.

Things don't always feel fair and just. We may feel compelled to stand up for ourselves, students, or a system that is constantly under fire. We face deadlines and administrative expectations that can be overwhelming. Many of us don't have job security or may be living paycheck to paycheck. In the face of all of these adversities, how do we enter the classroom, be with students, and teach with compassion?

Knowing how best to respond to adversity requires wisdom. And although we cannot sufficiently prepare for all that we may experience in any given school day, we can tap into our life experiences to help us navigate these daily difficulties in kind and thoughtful ways. Indeed, adversity, rather than being an obstacle to finding a pathway to compassion, can be a valuable portal, a practice ground, a way into the deeper understanding of our students and their behavior.

START WITH ADVERSITY, MOVE TO UNDERSTANDING

Compassion is closely linked to understanding. The word *understand* can be traced back to the Old English *understandan* meaning "to stand between or among." So, when we aspire to understand another, we stand among them. Similarly, when we are compassionate with another we stand with them in their suffering and seek to alleviate that suffering.

In *Tattoos on the Heart*, Father Gregory Boyle traces the understanding that fosters compassion to this notion of standing among others, which he calls "kinship." Of his work with gang members facing trauma, loss, and rage, Father Boyle explains, "You stand with the least likely to succeed until success is succeeded by something more valuable: kinship. You stand with the belligerent, the surly, and the badly behaved until bad behavior is recognized for the language it is: the vocabulary of the deeply wounded and of those whose burdens are more than they can bear."[1]

As we come to understand the lives of students and stand with them, particularly during times of adversity, we also come to understand the social context and conditions that they live within. In contrast, when we stand outside of others we tend to see them through our own limited perceptions, judge them based on our own experiences, and more easily attribute intentions to them that may be untrue, misguided, and misperceived.

When we position ourselves as outsiders, looking in, it is more difficult to understand what motivates a student's rage, disrespectful behavior, or seeming lack of care for learning. By standing with students we enter their worlds. We begin to understand the context behind their behavior and see that, in most cases, this behavior is a rational reaction to the circumstances that they face.

This does not mean that we condone violent or inappropriate behavior. It means that by standing with students, we have an opportunity to use moments of adversity as moments whereby we learn more about students, come to understand their suffering, and express our care and concern for their well-being. Such moments offer possibility and hope in the midst of pain and confusion.

Linda Cliatt-Wayman describes her experiences as a principal of Strawberry Mansion, a high school in north Philadelphia designated as "low performing and persistently dangerous." Her plan was to "lay down the law" and whip this school into shape.

Within hours of arriving for her first day there, a fight erupted in the halls. Cliatt-Wayman gathered the students and teachers into an assembly, preparing to dispatch her rules for appropriate conduct. Yet she was not prepared for what followed. A female student from the back of the room started scream-ing, "Miss, Miss . . ." After gaining the principal's attention, she shouted, "Why do you keep calling this a school? This is not a school."

This statement shocked Cliatt-Wayman into recognizing that all of her pre-conceived plans for creating law and order in the school were ill-conceived. She recalled her own experiences as a student in the same area of Philadel-phia, an area plagued by poverty and rampant violence and realized, that was not a school either: "When I look at them, I can only see what they can be-come. And that is because I am one of them. I grew up poor in north Philadel-phia, too. I know what it feels like to go to a school that's not a school. I know what it feels like to wonder if there's ever going to be a way out of poverty."[2]

Remembering that the key to her success, even amid so much adversity, was the understanding and love she received from her mother, Cliatt-Wayman began standing with her students, recognizing that they needed that love to succeed as well. Among many other changes that she instituted at the school, increased punishment was not one of them. Understanding their need for love, she ended every PA announcement with, "If no one told you they loved you today, remember I do, and I always will."

Within the first year of serving as principal, Strawberry Mansion was removed from the list of low-performing and persistently dangerous schools after having been on that list for the previous five consecutive years.

Cliatt-Wayman concludes,

> As we lead, we must never forget, that every single one of our students is just a child, often scared by what the world tells them they should be. And no matter what the rest of the world tells them they should be, we should always provide them with hope, our undivided attention, unwavering belief in their potential, consistent expectations, and we must tell them often if nobody told them they loved them today, remember we do, and we always will.[3]

UNDERSTANDING IS ROOTED IN SELF-COMPASSION

If your compassion does not include yourself, it is incomplete.

—Jack Kornfield

Self-compassion takes courage and a good deal of effort. As Paul Gilbert writes,

> If you think of people who are seen as very compassionate, such as Buddha, Christ, Nightingale, Gandhi, and Mandela, you'd hardly call them under-achievers. Developing self-compassion, therefore, is not simply a case of sitting around contemplating one's navel or just having nice thoughts about oneself. Developing self-compassion can be hard work and can inspire us to hard work.[4]

Or in the words of one of the author's autistic students who has been the object of much scorn and ridicule throughout his life: "Compassion is for the strong. The weak are either unable or unwilling to shoulder the pain of others."

As we do the hard work of developing self-compassion, our hearts expand, providing us with an ever-increasing capacity to offer compassion to others. This is particularly important during times when we ourselves face challenging situations. Kristen Neff, self-compassion researcher and teacher, shares her personal story of how her practice of self-compassion allowed her to be fully present and compassionate for her four-year-old autistic son.

While boarding a full plane heading to England, Neff's son began to throw a temper tantrum. Neff could sense other passengers' growing frustration and judgment as her son proceeded to yell and thrash about. She imagined them wondering why this seemingly normal child was acting so out of control. She further imagined the passengers wondering what was wrong with her for being unable to control her child. A sense of panic arose in Neff as she pondered what she should do.

Neff decided to take her son to the bathroom, hoping that would muffle her son's screams and give her a chance to help him calm down, yet the bathroom was occupied. As screams intensified and arms and legs flailed, she realized that the only thing she could do was to try to comfort herself. She attended to her fear and panic by putting her hands on her heart, and offered herself kind words, the sort of words that she would offer a friend facing troubling times. "This is so hard right now, darling. I'm so sorry that you're going through this, but I'm here for you," she said to herself.

Neff observed that by attending to her own anxiety, she remained openhearted to her son. As she shifted her reaction from fear to self-compassion and attended directly to her inner turmoil, her son's tantrum subsided. Neff remarks that many see this type of inner focus as selfish or self-indulgent. However, her experience and research suggest otherwise. Neff concludes, "The more we keep openhearted to ourselves the more we have available to give to others."[5]

Thirteenth-century German theologian Meister Eckhart makes a similar point, writing, "Thus the outer work can never be minor, when the inner work is a major one; and the outer work can never be major when the inner work is a minor one and without value."[6] When we put our energy into the inner work of developing self-compassion, we develop the resources, abilities, and energy to do the outer work of offering compassion to others.

And developing self-compassion is not always easy; it requires our effort. We can all recall times as teachers when something went wrong: we said something that triggered another's anger, we felt embarrassed in front of a large group, we lost the attention of the students and chaos ensued, we reacted with annoyance instead of patience as a student muttered an inarticulate excuse for late homework. In such instances, we may quickly turn on ourselves and even beat ourselves up for not responding in a different or more compassionate manner.

To learn from adversity we have to be willing to experience it and direct compassion inward. When we ignore challenging emotions that arise during teaching and throughout our work as educators, we become prone to bitterness, resentment, and spitefulness. As one educator remarked, "I know too many teachers who are passive aggressive." Such negative states may be due, in part, to a lack of opportunities to recognize, address, and cultivate self-compassion amid the real stresses and strains inherent in our work.

Regrettably, there is a dearth of opportunities and structures in place for educators to attend to and address the emotions that arise during challenging experiences. Some schools do offer teachers counseling, wellness programs, continuing education classes, and workshops that focus on stress management, health, and well-being. Yet by and large, there are few institutional structures built into the educational system designed explicitly to help educators address these strong feelings.

Fortunately, we can draw on the wisdom of people like Tara Brach, psychologist and Buddhist educator. She uses a practical tool for effectively working with and responding to the strong feelings that emerge with adversity. The tool is called RAIN[7]—*R* for Recognize, *A* for Attend, *I* for Investigate, *N* for Nonidentification and Natural awareness.

RECOGNIZE ADVERSITY: THE *R* IN RAIN

So often we experience negative feelings and states of mind and ignore them, push them to the back of our minds, or dismiss them as invalid. This only offers our distress comfortable hiding places where it can lurk, more than ready to arise again when the circumstances present themselves. Only by recognizing and naming our difficult emotions can we shine the light of awareness upon them, keep them exposed and vulnerable to scrutiny, so we can deal with them directly. Ultimately, our troubled states of mind, painful emotions, and other forms of distress and dis-ease simply want our attention and healing.

As teachers, we all experience frustration and anger from time to time. It may be a few disruptive students who sour the culture of the classroom, colleagues who seem to put in the least amount of effort, or administrators who treat teachers with scorn and disrespect. Yet, as the chapter-opening observation by Marvin Ashton reminds us, how we attend to adversity makes all the difference.

When we are angry a part of us suffers, and we look for relief from this suffering. Some find relief by blaming others for their suffering. Some seek relief through releasing their anger onto another. In an educational setting, perhaps this is best illustrated when a teacher yells at a student. Some find relief through self-blame or self-pity. Some suppress anger. However, rather than simply reacting to adverse situations or suppressing our rage, we can recognize and attend to our inner experience in the present moment.

Rosanne, a community-college instructor, often took the risk of using her own life experiences, including her experience as a lesbian, to help students understand inequalities of race, class, gender, and sexual orientation. One day, while sharing a story about a time when she and her partner were poorly treated in a restaurant, a student shouted a slur about lesbians from the back of the classroom. Rosanne felt her heart sink and her face turn red as she felt the familiar sting of homophobia strike her. She took a deep breath and instead of trying to minimize the event, she forced herself to acknowledge she felt angry and hurt.

She attributes her ability to compose herself, invite the student to talk with her after class, and continue on with the lesson to the simple act of openly acknowledging to herself the pain he had caused. If she hadn't, she says, she most likely would have verbally lashed out at him. By recognizing how she felt within, Rosanne was able to respond rather than react impulsively to the situation and remain professional, dignified, and focused on teaching.

ATTENDING TO DIFFICULT EMOTIONS: THE *A* IN RAIN

Thich Nhat Hanh advises us to attend to our anger as we would a baby. He writes,

> Embrace your anger with a lot of tenderness. Your anger is not your enemy, your anger is your baby. It's like your stomach or your lungs. Every time you have some trouble in your lungs or your stomach, you don't think of throwing them away. The same is true with your anger. You accept your anger because you know you can take care of it; you can transform it into positive energy.[8]

Anger demonstrates some type of need we have within ourselves. Perhaps it is a need to be understood, respected, or loved. We can attend to our anger as we would attend to a hurt child. We can listen to our anger. We can talk with our anger. We can offer comfort to our anger.

Recognizing and attending can happen in a moment. This does not have to be a long and laborious process. Nor do we have to wait for the right moment to attend to adverse experiences, although developing practices that help us recognize and attend to adversity while we are not in the heat of the moment can help us during times of strife and hardship. The following exercise is designed to help educators develop this practice.

❧

EXERCISE: ATTENDING TO ADVERSITY

Bring to mind a time when you reacted negatively to a challenging situation in the classroom. Recall the moment before you reacted, when your anger was seething or the frustration was growing. See if you can recall this experience, not just in your mind, but in your body. Where in your body were you tight? Was your heart racing? Try to reenact the way you felt as you faced this challenging situation.

Play out the scene all the way to the point where you reacted. Now, instead of getting lost in your feeling, identify your feeling and talk with it in a kind, caring, compassionate manner. Thich Nhat Hanh suggests something like, "My dear anger [or whatever strong feeling it is] I know you are there. I am taking good care of you."[9] What kind and gentle words feel natural to you? Try talking with yourself with as much love and care as you can evoke.

Practicing this kind of communication is like exercising your self-compassion muscle. So when you are in the midst of a challenging situation, you are already accustomed to attending to the difficult emotions that arise within. Eventually this type of attending to yourself through compassionate self-talk becomes a natural and automatic response during adverse times.

We recognize that positive self-talk may not be for everyone. However, consider all the negative self-talk many of us do, if not often, at least some of the time. Do any of these negative internal messages sound familiar to you?

- I'm not qualified enough to teach this class.
- There's no use in trying to get through to these students. Why would they listen to me?
- I can't do this anymore!
- I'm such a procrastinator. Why didn't I prepare better?
- I'm not one of those charismatic teachers that students love. Students won't like me.

- The other teachers are smarter than me.
- I'm not good enough.
- What I have to offer doesn't really matter.
- I'm hopeless! When will I ever learn from my mistakes?

What narratives stream through your mind? When facing hardship, what do you tell yourself? Do you tell yourself how much you care for yourself and how you will get through this? Or do you berate yourself for having not done a better job or for not being a more mindful and compassionate teacher? How might shifting negative self-narratives impact your ability to be compassionate to others during times of adversity, particularly when facing challenging situations as a teacher?

INVESTIGATING ADVERSITY: THE *I* IN RAIN

We can also try to understand the roots of our own afflictive states. The philosopher and poet David Whyte suggests that anger is not merely a negative emotion of animosity, fury, and rage that needs to be transformed; instead, anger is the deepest expression of compassion.[10] If we didn't care about students' emotional, social, and intellectual well-being then we wouldn't get angry at the countless forces that seem to conspire against them.

Compassion can indeed manifest as anger just as love can manifest as anxiety. There may be no greater sense of adversity as when we feel simultaneously committed to our mission as educators and helpless about our ability to carry out this mission. As a result, we may feel a sense of righteous indignation or, in a word, anger.

When understood as a response to that which we care about, the anger we experience as teachers demonstrates to us our deep commitment to education. It brings us back to this commitment even in the midst of seemingly insurmountable obstacles. None of us ever lash out at something to which we are indifferent. If a loved one is hurt, if a student has been wronged, or if we feel disrespected, we may express anger because we have genuine love and concern for the object of pain and suffering. If we are willing to investigate and understand the roots of our anger, then it can serve as a great teacher helping us to clarify our principles, touch our suffering, and ultimately inspire us to construct more altruistic practices.

☙❧

EXERCISE: INVESTIGATING ADVERSITY

The following exercises can be used to gain a deeper understanding of adversity in ourselves or others. The first version of this exercise is intended to help you understand another by entering another's world through your senses and imagination, to see how close you can come to feeling what they may be feeling. The second version is intended to help you understand your own challenging emotions through investigating how emotions reside within your body. This is a very different sort of investigation than many of us are used to doing as teachers and academics. By *investigate* we do not mean using our minds to analyze our experience; rather, we turn within to investigate how the adverse experiences manifest in the body, our own and others'.

James Joyce's classic line, Mr. Duffy "lived at a little distance from his body"[11] mirrors what many educators, us included, experience throughout much of our careers—a distancing from our bodies, often lost in our minds, and ultimately believing our minds (or someone else's mind) can provide us with all the answers we seek. Both exercises help us develop an embodied understanding of adversity—an understanding that links body, heart, and mind.

Version 1: Investigating Adversity within Another

This exercise guides us to investigate how another person may feel by putting ourselves in their shoes. We try to imagine what they feel as if we are going through the experience ourselves.

This exercise is best conducted after having observed negative behavior in another. After witnessing another's negative behavior (for example, a student acting disruptively in the classroom) try to recall their nonverbal behaviors. Does their jaw seem tight? Does their body language suggest they are wound tightly? Try to imagine what this student feels like by adopting their nonverbal behaviors. Clench your jaw and constrict your body.

The point is to feel from within what it feels like to be so keyed up. Do your best to feel from within all of the behaviors you perceived in another. Notice what emotions emerge. Take your time to investigate the different areas of your body. It is useful to even emulate the actions and positions of the student. If the student was slumping, be sure to slump. If the student was scowling, be sure to scowl. Ask yourself, how does it feel to be like this?

As you investigate what the student might be going through by observing the feelings within your body, notice any emotions that you feel. Perhaps in this position with slumped back, clenched jaw, tight fists, and so forth, you begin feeling a lot of anger within your own body. What insights emerge from this experience? In the example, you may gain an embodied understanding of how much anger this student is holding and what it feels like to be in a body seething with rage. See what understanding and insights arise by embodying the behaviors you noticed in another.

The point here is to figuratively place oneself in the shoes of another. As you simulate the physical sensations of this other person, you may begin to gain greater understanding and insight into the difficulties they face. This in turn can help you connect with and be responsive to the pain and suffering they may be experiencing.

Version 2: Investigating Adversity within Ourselves

This exercise is designed to help you investigate how your own challenging emotions feel within your body. Begin by recognizing and naming your emotional state. Now turn within and notice where these emotions reside in your body. For example, if you feel frustrated with a student, maybe your jaw clenches or your stomach tightens. If you feel undermined by a colleague, perhaps your head begins to pound. If you feel disrespected by an administrator, maybe you feel a burning sensation in your heart.

Not only can we investigate where within our bodies our emotions reside, but we can also observe how our emotions actually feel in our bodies. Notice the associated physical sensations: heat, throbbing, tightness, or burning sensations as they course through your body. You can also watch the lifespan of your emotions, how they shift, morph, and eventually dissipate—sometimes faster than expected.

Pay attention to the way emotions live within your body. Observe what thoughts are associated with the varying sensations of your body. As you investigate how challenging emotions live in your body, note any insights or understanding that emerge.

PRACTICING NONIDENTIFICATION: THE *N* IN RAIN

Developing a practice of nonidentification allows us to release ourselves from the habit of attaching our sense of self to passing experiences. Simply put, we take fewer things personally. Tara Brach explains, "Non-identification means that your sense of who you are is not fused with or defined by any limited set of emotions, sensations, or stories. When identification with the small self is loosened, we begin to intuit and live from the openness and love that express our natural awareness."[12]

Nonidentification is a choice. Thich Nhat Hanh teaches that when we water the seeds of kindness and compassion, these qualities grow and flourish within us. Conversely, when we water the seeds of ill will, greed, and delusion, these qualities grow and flourish in us and others.

Neuroscientist and author Rick Hanson shares a Native American elder's response when asked how she became so wise, happy, and respected: "In my heart, there are two wolves: a wolf of love and a wolf of hate. It all depends on which one I feed each day."[13]

If we've been feeding the wolf of hate, we are more likely to face hardship with bitterness, anger, and hostility. If we have been feeding the wolf of love, we are more likely to face hardship with patience, calm, and compassion. To transform adversity into compassionate teaching we may feed the wolf of love, nourishing the qualities and creating the conditions out of which compassion arises. Hanson offers this advice: "Be careful about the intentions you attribute to others; take fewer things personally; regard your ill will as an affliction upon yourself that you naturally want to be relieved of; resolve to meet mistreatment with loving-kindness; communicate and assert yourself; and forgive."[14]

Let's look at these recommendations one by one and explore how each may help us transform adversity and support our capacity to teach with compassion.

1. Be Careful about the Intentions You Attribute to Others

Have you ever found yourself creating a story in your mind about a student or colleague, only later to realize that what you thought motivated that person's actions was completely untrue, misguided, and ultimately misperceived?

We see, for example, bored students disrupting class through restless and impatient behavior. When teachers attribute mischievous or even malicious intentions to these disruptions, they blind themselves to other possibilities, for example, that the student may be frustrated with his or her own lack of understanding. Parker Palmer's insights about the Student from Hell archetype are instructive here: "We need a new diagnosis of our students' inward condition, one that is more perceptive about their needs, less defensive about our own role in their plight, and more likely to lead to creative modes of teaching."[15]

It seems crucial that we acknowledge the intentions we attribute to students, recognizing when we project our own ideas about their behaviors onto them.

Compassion arises when we spend time not only identifying our own projections and assumptions, but also getting to know and understand students.

2. Take Fewer Things Personally

While we may place a good deal of time and energy into lesson planning, take faculty development or continuing education workshops and classes, try to learn from our errors, and so forth, the dynamics of a classroom are fraught with unlimited forces and conditions. It's not simply because of us that a particular class, for example, goes well or poorly. The dynamics and combination of student personalities, our and our students' moods and experiences on a particular day, even the cultural tides and our relationships with others have unseen influences.

[handwritten margin note: factors out of your control]

As social network analysis reveals and as further discussed in the book's conclusion, our friends and our friends' friends influence our behaviors and experiences in unexpected ways.[16] *(ie: US and (Students))*

Taking fewer things personally, acknowledging the complex, sometimes known but often unknown, dynamics at play relieves us of assuming that everything that goes poorly is our fault and everything that goes well is our success. As we take fewer things personally we may continue to hone our skills while humbly appreciating our contributions to creating more compassionate learning environments.

3. Regard Your Ill Will as an Affliction upon Yourself That You Naturally Want to Be Relieved Of

We feel the corrosive effects of ill will, often expressed as anger and hatred, within ourselves. Anger has a direct and visceral feeling; we can directly experience our bodies heat up as we literally boil within. Hatred and, perhaps more germane to how we may feel about some students and colleagues, dislike can have a more simmering long-lasting effect and also manifest physically as illness within us.

Ill will is ultimately so painful that we naturally wish to be relieved of it. We wish for external factors to change—wishing the year to be over so that we no longer have to deal with *that* student or wishing the student would maybe realize the class isn't for her and simply go away. To tame this wolf of ill will, we can observe how it feels within us and move toward a natural desire to alleviate suffering. Rather than looking to change external factors, we can look within. The exercises throughout this chapter are designed to help us do this.

4. Resolve to Meet Mistreatment with Loving-Kindness

The term *loving-kindness* derives from the Buddhist practice of metta, translated as loving-kindness, but also meaning benevolence, friendliness, goodwill, and kindness. This does not mean that we should allow ourselves to be victims of another's abusive behavior; rather, it means that we wish well even to those who mistreat us. We recognize that abuse is always rooted in suffering. When we meet mistreatment with kindness, we have an opportunity to diffuse another's anger and provide a chance for healing to take place.

At the time of this writing, university professors across the country have experienced a stream of cyberbullying instigated by students accusing their professors of inserting their own politics into the classroom. The students post comments on social media, often on websites designed to mobilize mass action, and then the professors' email inboxes get bombarded with messages, often of an extremely threatening nature. This creates deep anguish in these professors' lives, sometimes to the point where they fear for their lives.

Having witnessed this happen to some of our colleagues, we've been struck by how many of them have practiced a type of metta—they have treated the offending student with kindness and respect. One faculty member made it her practice to continue to express goodwill toward a student who instigated a particularly vicious cyberattack on her. By the end of the semester the student—whose social media posts mobilized thousands of people to bombard the professor's inbox with hateful emails—thanked our colleague for her unwavering kindness and expressed deep regret for the pain and suffering she caused.

Metta is regarded in Buddhism as the most powerful remedy for taming the wolves of hate and anger. When we address another's anger with anger, we fuel the fire of anger. Loving-kindness and genuine friendliness produce neither vengeful feelings nor fuel anger and hatred.

5. Communicate and Assert Yourself

Lest we be concerned that expressing kindness and compassion leaves us vulnerable to be preyed upon and devoured by the wolves of hate or students waiting to take advantage of our kindness, Hanson offers another tool to be combined with compassion: assertion. He explains, "Compassion widens the circle of 'us' while assertion protects and supports everyone inside it. They both nourish the wolf of love."[17] To illustrate this, Hanson shares his observations of meditation teachers' behaviors at board meetings that he attended over a nine-year period:

They were compassionate about the concerns of others, but when they said what they thought, they did so clearly and often strongly, without hemming and hawing. And then they let it be, not becoming defensive or argumentative. This combination of openheartedness and directness was very powerful. It got the job done while nurturing the love in the room.[18]

6. Forgive

Wrongs may have been committed. Students may say inappropriate things. We may react unmindfully (and find it challenging to forgive ourselves). Colleagues may act unprofessionally. We may act unprofessionally. The list goes on. We all make mistakes. Hanson explains, "Forgiveness doesn't mean changing your view that wrongs have been done. But it does mean letting go of the emotional charge around feeling wronged. The greatest beneficiary of your forgiveness is usually you."[19]

Through forgiveness we hold each other accountable and transform the desire to punish into the desire to heal hurtful and abusive patterns. Aurora Levins Morales's profound insights into forgiveness are especially relevant here. In *Medicine Stories* Morales writes that we undermine our vision of a compassionate world when we reject the parts of our world that are most wounded. Forgiving even those who have most hurt and enraged us is a healing process.

Using the example of torturers, Morales explains, "The urge to punish, to execute, to wipe them out is the refusal to consider what we ourselves might be capable of."[20] Through forgiveness we recognize within ourselves the wounds that drive another to behave as they do. Through this recognition, we not only have an opportunity to heal our own shame, but we also have an opportunity to recognize the humanity and healing potential within another. In the case of students and colleagues, through forgiveness we create transformative possibilities for healing, learning, and growth.

EXERCISE: NONIDENTIFICATION
AND NATURAL AWARENESS

Nonidentification can be cultivated by taking a moment every day to practice natural awareness. Natural awareness is a kind of mindfulness practice; however, instead of the traditional mindfulness practice of focusing on the breath as an anchor into present-moment awareness—practices we explore in more depth in the final chapter of the book—try shifting your attention to the part of you that does the noticing, the part that notices thoughts, emotions, sensations. In other words, try shifting your focus to awareness itself.

Here are two exercises that can help you build the capacity to rest in natural awareness. They are simple. The hard part is making the commitment to doing them every day. Over time you will begin to notice a difference in your awareness.

1. Take three conscious breaths and then focus on the part of you that notices that breath. This is awareness itself. Rest here for a few moments before entering the classroom.

2. Set an intention to notice frustration when it arises in or out of the classroom. When you notice frustration arising, focus on the part of you that notices the frustration. This is natural awareness. As Jon Kabat-Zinn explains, this connects you to the part of you that is aware of the frustration (or illness, anger, etc.) and is itself not frustrated.[21]

And just a reminder, as with all the practices shared in this book, please be gentle and compassionate with yourself. While we encourage you to try out these practices, we also recommend that if something does not feel right or feels too frustrating, just let it go or try again another time.

Through a process of contemplation and shifting our inner narratives, our perceptions of adverse situations begin to shift. Eventually, we may even forgive those who hurt us. We can recognize that wrongs have been committed, but in time, we learn to loosen our grip on the emotional charge. Rather than fixating on our anger, we may wonder what conditions would lead someone to act in such a hurtful manner. This sense of curiosity for another's life conditions gives the wolf of love a little something to nibble on.

QUESTIONS FOR FURTHER REFLECTION

1. What are the most challenging situations you currently face as a teacher? How might practicing RAIN help you compassionately address these challenges?

2. What gets you most angry in your daily life as an educator? In what ways might this anger represent a form of compassion?

3. What does your inner voice say to you during challenging times in the classroom? Do you have a strong and active "inner critic"? What are one or two phrases you could say to yourself to practice compassionate self-talk?

4. Identify a negative judgment that you have about a student or colleague. What may you be overlooking, or not understanding, about that person's adverse behaviors? What is one thing you could do to "stand among them" and foster further understanding?

5. In your daily teaching life, what are some ways that you feed the wolf of hate? What are some ways that you feed the wolf of love and compassion? What is one thing that you could do to tame the wolf of hate and feed the wolf of love?

Chapter Four

Leave My Ego at the Door

Through humility and a sense of vulnerability, I bring an open and welcoming heart to my teaching.

During the first week of classes, Janine asks students to get into small groups and share stories about some of the best class discussions they have experienced and come up with a list of the top elements that facilitate successful discussions (the template for this exercise can be found in chapter 7, "Hold Space"). One semester a group of students listed "Leave your ego at the door!" as their number one ingredient. Janine knew immediately that the students were onto something important that had implications beyond holding good discussions, an insight so obvious and useful she was surprised she hadn't thought of it before.

How many times have you finished a lesson thinking that you really nailed it? Maybe you created an activity in which everyone seemed to participate eagerly, handed out an assignment that students did not want to stop working on, or explained a complex and confusing concept in a clear and illuminating manner?

We may use moments like these as self-congratulatory confirmations that we have indeed solved the riddle of teaching. We feel buoyed that we are masters of our craft. That is, until we go home at night and read what students actually wrote, test them on the concepts we just taught, or talk to students who were sitting in the back of the room. Only then do we realize that not everyone participated, that some students were not working on the assignment but were engrossed in their own activity, and that a good portion of students were just pretending to understand that abstract idea because they were too self-conscious, maybe even too afraid, to ask for further elucidation.

How quickly the rug gets pulled out from under us, serving us a nice big piece of humble pie (excuse the mixed metaphor!). At first, we may not welcome its appearance at our table. After all, many of us have come to believe that we *do* have all of the answers—if not in our heads then at least in the annotated teacher's text. But such smugness and arrogance only lead us down dead ends. But it is in such moments of reckoning that we are fully alive to our roles as teachers, when we are learning and must go back to the drawing board and return our focus to what matters: our students.

This oath point, Leave My Ego at the Door, builds on an idea we began exploring in the first chapter on beginner's mind, that teaching with compassion means finding a way to teach from a place of humility, and at times, vulnerability. It means considering the "big picture" needs of students and prioritizing their growth, development, and well-being over our own needs for validation and approval.

Leaving our egos at the door paradoxically requires enough confidence in our teaching and in ourselves to put aside any need to prove ourselves or demonstrate our knowledge. It requires us to step off the pedestals that many of us have spent our careers building up, admit that we do not have all of the answers even when we are often expected to know everything, and enter into a more engaged relationship with students, one that allows us to meet students where they are, attune ourselves to their learning styles, help them make meaningful connections to course materials, and discover how to best facilitate the development of their skills. At the same time we dismantle, or at least diminish, the emotional blockades we have put in place that inhibit students from seeing us as fully human.

The importance of setting off on this path cannot be overstated. As noted in the introduction and as Karen Armstrong states, compassion is not possible unless we "dethrone ourselves from the center of our world" and embrace "our common humanity" with others. Teaching with compassion, then, is also not possible if we cling stubbornly to our cherished sense of self.

WHAT IS EGO?

There is no physical entity that we may identify and label as *ego*. Historically, philosophers, psychologists, and scientists have searched for this one central organizing structure in the brain and have come up short. Still, we have a sense of self, a sense that someone with specific experiences, perceptions, thoughts, emotions, and sensations is running the show.

Sigmund Freud maintained that the ego is the part of the psyche that mediates the desires of the id (instincts) with the inner critique and moralism of the superego. The ego is the part of us that organizes our experiences and provides us with a sense of self. This way of thinking about the ego concretizes it into an entity that, although unseen, still exists and runs our lives. Over time the term has been popularized and equated with self-esteem and from here we find such terms as *swollen ego*, *egotistic*, and *egomania*, all referring to an inflated sense of self—one that perceives itself as better than others.

Teaching is based in a relationship between self and others, a reciprocal process, in which how we interact with others matters. When our actions are guided by the dictates of the ego, either by blindly asserting our authority or making decisions based on what might make us look good rather than what will serve the interest of students, we are defining the educational experience in terms of ourselves. When we interact with students with openness and receptivity, with genuine concern for their well-being and interest in who they are as people, however, we create a different educational environment and open up exciting possibilities for learning.

Yet, it is not like we can just hang up our egos on hooks before entering a classroom. Rather, we first need to spend time identifying the way our egos drive some of our self-protective or unproductive behaviors so we can begin to dismantle them. Here is a brief exercise designed to offer a sense of how you may begin leaving your ego at the door.

⊙⅋ɕ⅋

EXERCISE: THREE STEPS TO IDENTIFY
AND DROP YOUR EGO

Step 1: Identify three ways that your ego "runs the show" when teaching. It may help to think about recent choices you made as a teacher—maybe how you responded to a student, perhaps a student who was misbehaving or one who asked for a favor. Or there may be ways you've sought out positive words of validation from a colleague or even a student. Maybe you view the classroom as a stage to display your knowledge or exert influence. To what degree did a concern about how you would look to others factor into your choices?

Step 2: Place yourself in the position of a particular student in your classroom. From this student's perspective, write down a response to the following prompt: "Three things my teacher could do to leave her/his ego at the door are _____."

Step 3: Merge steps 1 and 2 and ask yourself, <u>What could I do to enter the classroom with less of an ego and greater openness to the students' perspectives, knowledge, and wisdom?</u>

EGOLESS COMPASSION

Many of us believe that with the right intentions we will do right by students. But egos can be tricky. Even thinking of oneself as a compassionate teacher may reinforce a type of ego blindness. We become so busy playing a role that we don't actually see students, sense their struggles, or understand their needs. The key is to work toward what we call *egoless compassion*, driven less by our own ambition and self-image and more by an <u>authentic interest and care for the lives, well-being, and development of others.</u> Let's consider the following example.

Ms. Gruwell was a young and idealistic English teacher who took pride in her commitment to compassion. Determined to "change the world" and to right wrongs, she found herself one day responding in righteous anger after intercepting a caricature that reminded her of Nazi propaganda of Jews and challenged her class with a question: "How many of you have ever been shot?" With this one question, she opened up the floodgates. Scars were revealed and harrowing stories were shared of violent lives. Ms. Gruwell explains what she learned that day:

> Every kid has a story. . . . I handed out notebooks for my students to journal about their lives. There was some initial resistance. But then the stories poured out of them, <u>full of anger and sadness</u>. They wrote about sexual abuse, gang violence, hurt and hate. Many of them were stories they hadn't told anyone. It wasn't just the writing, but hearing and editing each other's stories was cathartic for my students, really a profound healing process. Once they began to write their own stories, it opened them up to the possibility of being able to rewrite their endings.[1]

Ms. Gruwell, her heart, eyes, and ears newly opened to the stories of these students' real experiences, was suddenly able to see them as individuals, so much more than so-called at-risk and troubled youth. She was moved to let go of her vision of herself as a social crusader and throw herself into the work of making the classroom a place where all students knew they were welcome. She did such things as cover the walls with snapshots of the students and made it a place they could always come to before and after school. Their real lives provided the fodder for them to learn, grow, express, teach, and be accepted as they were.

These students' stories ultimately became a *New York Times* best seller and a motion picture, *The Freedom Writers Diary*. Compassion rooted in a deep caring for others rather than in the maintenance of one's egoistic identity undoubtedly played a role in helping all 150 of Ms. Gruwell's students graduate from high school.

BLAMING AND ACCEPTING RESPONSIBILITY[2]

Most teachers can relate to the feeling of anxiety that arises at the beginning of the year when we walk into a new classroom and encounter difficult students. We brace ourselves in anticipation of the challenge to our classroom management skills that we know will come. But, perhaps more important, we brace ourselves also for the inevitable beating our self-image as competent professionals will undergo. How can we meet this challenge without letting our egos get in the way of making the best, most compassionate choices as a teacher? How can we meet it without falling into a destructive cycle of blaming?

Hannah, a high school history teacher, recently faced this question head on. Over the years, she had viewed these students as problems and developed internal strategies for dealing with them. As she tells the story now, she sees that she had created and reinforced an antagonistic relationship, blaming certain students for creating a negative classroom environment, defending and protecting her sense of self, and inevitably feeling a tense grip overcome her as she walked into a classroom occupied by an abrasive student.

Fortunately, Hannah wasn't comfortable with this relationship. She knew she had to make a change. She had been reading about compassion and began reflecting more fully on her approaches to teaching. Inspired by Karen Armstrong's call for us to *treat everybody, without exception, with absolute justice, equity, and respect,* she made a decision. She turned her attention to a problem student she had identified in her new class, the one who sneered at her and rolled his eyes as she introduced the class expectations. This student was not seriously disruptive, just unmotivated and grumbly.

Rather than trying to simply put up with the student over the year she would give him the same attention she gave to her most beloved students. Before stepping in the classroom every day, she took a moment to remind herself of her new intention. From an outsider's perspective, one probably could not see a shift in Hannah's behavior, but she was careful to smile at the disaffected student and wherever possible, offer positive feedback, focusing on his strengths. After a few weeks of classes this student began lighting up as he entered the classroom, began taking on leadership roles in the classroom, worked hard, and by the end of the school year had become one of the highest achieving students in the class.

What might we learn from this example? We may begin to identify the students that we wish would just disappear and bring interest and genuine kindness to our interactions with them. This may take on many different forms, depending on the needs of each student. In some cases, it means establishing rapport with the student through direct interaction like asking the student how they are doing that day or complimenting the student on something they did well. In other cases, bringing genuine kindness to our interactions with the student may mean offering a simple smile or internally wishing them well.

We may also recognize that students behave in direct response to their unique life situations. Rather than judging them and setting up protective barriers, our intention should be to facilitate their understanding and learning. Furthermore, as we begin to understand the ways in which we have developed a sense of self, one that needs defending and shoring up, we can begin to take responsibility for our role in creating negative dynamics.

Taking responsibility for our role in creating negative dynamics does not justify abusive behavior from students (see the discussion on creating boundaries in chapter 7, "Hold Space," for more about this). However, it does mean that we should take note of the aversion we feel toward some students and seek ways of engaging more fully with them. We can begin to release some of the patterns of behavior that separate us from each other and open ourselves up to opportunities for connection. From here learning becomes a truly collaborative venture.

Playing the blame game is not unusual; in fact, it is prevalent throughout educational settings. If we drew a diagram of the blame game among students, teachers, administrators, parents, government officials, and media pundits, we would have an intricate web of condemnation.

The one thing that would be ostensibly missing from such a diagram is any sort of feedback loop that brought the blame back to the original party that felt wronged. Although there are countless problems with education today, and just as many scapegoats, it is exceedingly rare to find anyone willing to assume responsibility for the troubles they have identified.

In listening to teachers over the years we have heard all sorts of complaints but the most common ones seem to revolve around three themes: students' lack of civility in the classroom (texting on cell phones, sleeping, talking with friends, being rude); their unwillingness to do the work (not handing in as-

*venting
not use to colleagues* [handwritten annotation in top margin]

signments, coming to class unprepared); and their unabashed use of academically dishonest tactics (plagiarizing, making cheat sheets, copying answers from each other). These are indeed real issues that should not be taken lightly.

But our venting to colleagues, as tempting as it is, will not rectify these issues. The first step is to seriously consider how we may have contributed to these problems. Leaving our egos at the door means being willing to see where we can do better as teachers and as educators. Where do we unintentionally create the conditions that promote these undesirable behaviors?

If students are ignorant perhaps our teaching methods require rethinking. If they are disengaged, maybe we can do more to spark interest and reinforce the relevance of the material. And if they are cheating, perhaps we need to rethink how we are assessing learning.

The point here, however, is not to accept total responsibility for everything that occurs in the classroom; certainly, some accountability rests with learners. What we can strive for is recognizing that problems students experience are *our* problems too because we are co-creators of the educational process.

If we drop our ego-protecting suit of armor and expose ourselves to potentially uncomfortable realizations about ourselves, then we can learn many lessons. We allow ourselves to become truly reflective practitioners, capable of seriously interrogating long-standing and cherished strategies that may no longer—or may never have—served us, our colleagues, or our students well. Teachers may learn that their lectures are dull; administrators may recognize that their management style is overbearing; and students may realize that their behavior is immature. But these realizations will not occur unless we are receptive to them.

❧☙

EXERCISE: SHIFTING AWAY FROM JUDGMENT AND BLAME

This exercise is based on a process of inquiry called The Work. Developed by author Byron Katie it helps participants explore judgments, blames, and taken-for-granted assumptions, providing a toolkit for shifting away from blame and judgment into a more generative space of acceptance and possibility. Following is an abbreviated version of The Work designed for teaching with compassion.

Step 1: Identify a judgment. For example: Students are narrow-minded.

Step 2: Answer the following four questions, allowing yourself to be honest and thoughtful about your responses:

1. Is my judgment true? (Yes or no. If no, move to question 3.) *Example:* Is it true that students are narrow-minded?
2. Can you absolutely know that it's true? (Yes or no) *Example:* Can you absolutely know that it's true that students are narrow-minded?
3. How do you react when you believe that thought? *Example:* How do you react when you believe the thought that students are narrow-minded?
4. How would you act without the thought? *Example:* How would you act differently toward students if you didn't believe they were narrow-minded?

Step 3: Identify a turnaround. A turnaround is a statement that is opposite the original judgment. For example, for the judgment "Students are narrow-minded," a turnaround could be "I am narrow-minded." Then ask, could this turnaround be true or even truer than the original judgment? For example, could it be true that "I am narrow-minded"? Perhaps the judgment "Students are narrow-minded" is itself a narrow way of looking at students.

Step 4: Contemplate new possibilities. For example, perhaps you come to realize that students by their nature do come to our classes with a certain amount of narrow-mindedness. That's why they are ostensibly getting an education—to learn and to grow. We can even reconnect with our original purposes for becoming teachers: to open up minds, offer new perspectives, create opportunities for others, and so forth. The point is to realize that through judgment and blame we easily escape responsibility and close ourselves off from the possibilities of bringing an open and creative heart to our teaching.

VULNERABILITY AND ACCEPTANCE

The term *vulnerable* derives from the Latin verb *vulnerare*, which means "to wound, hurt, injure, or maim." When we feel vulnerable, we fear being hurt by another. And often to protect ourselves from being hurt or injured we project a sense of invulnerability or an inflated ego.

Yet when we build walls of invulnerability around ourselves—fortresses of protection—we make it very hard for others to connect with us. And while protecting our egos from pain may feel better than opening ourselves up and feeling our wounds, invariably such ego protecting keeps the world at arm's length. By covering up our vulnerabilities and being unwilling to feel our insecurities, we may hide behind a veneer of authority or intellectualism. By

Don't close these doors [handwritten marginal note]

leaving our egos at the door and allowing vulnerability in, we move toward becoming more compassionate educators willing to feel and connect.

This process also aids in our own self-development. In her book of essays, *Teaching to Transgress*, feminist educator bell hooks points out how important it is that we willingly welcome in ourselves the same sort of susceptibility and openness that we often expect from students: "Any classroom that employs a holistic model of learning will also be a place where teachers grow, and are empowered by the process. That empowerment cannot happen if we refuse to be vulnerable while encouraging students to take risks."[3]

Embracing vulnerability is no easy task. As teachers, we are acutely aware that our flaws are on display to students, administrators, and colleagues. Some of us may experience a kind of "imposter syndrome" whereby even as confidence grows with experience, there remains a gnawing sense that somehow, magically, we've fooled the world into thinking we know what we're doing.

We have a choice. We can cover up and hide, fleeing from our sense of vulnerability, or we can express the fullness of who we are, flaws and all, and begin to accept our human limitations. We can face not only the limits of our knowledge but also our less-than-stellar behaviors. Who among us has been kind 100 percent of the time? Who has responded to life's demands and challenging people with total equanimity and understanding?

Tara Brach, whose work with RAIN we discussed in chapter 3, "Learn from Adversity," describes how through a process of "radical acceptance" we can embrace our blunders and imperfections and learn to face them head on. Brach explains that with radical acceptance we are willing "to experience ourselves and our life as it is. A moment of radical acceptance is a moment of genuine freedom."[4] The heart expands and compassion organically grows as we identify, accept, and love ourselves and others.

To experience ourselves and our lives as they are is also to be vulnerable. If we are to really accept ourselves and others in this way we must face our deeper fears and wounds and in so doing, according to Brach, "discover that our heart of compassion widens endlessly."[5] Yet, we tend to reinforce our egos as a way of protecting ourselves from being vulnerable.

Poet and philosopher David Whyte builds on this point by noting, "To run from vulnerability is to run from the essence of our nature, the attempt to be invulnerable is the vain attempt to become something we are not and most especially, to close off our understanding of the grief of others."[6] For many of us, our egos become citadels against the discomfort of becoming vulnerable.

As we accept our own limitations and vulnerabilities, we can accept the limitations and vulnerabilities of students. This does not mean that we cease challenging students. We have known for a long time that student success depends on setting and communicating high expectations.[7] Accepting the limitations of students means that we recognize they are learners (as are we all); they have not perfected their understanding. Students may be skilled in certain areas while deficient in others.

How can we respond to students with encouragement while providing necessary constructive feedback? We might ask ourselves: What most assisted us when we fell short? Certainly, it was not being offered uncritical approval (being given an A for simply handing in work). Nor did any of us improve and learn by being chastised or simply given a low or failing grade with little or no feedback. Our best teachers provide us with unconditional acceptance, appreciate us as we are—flaws and all—while trusting that we have more to offer. They help us express, in Brach's words, the "fullness of who we are."[8]

Great teachers support us in our growth and development, they accept us with all of our unseen and unspoken flaws, and they see and mirror for us *more*. As American lama in the Tibetan tradition and author Lama Surya Das writes in his book *Make Me One with Everything: Buddhist Meditations to Awaken from the Illusion of Separation*, great teachers *educe*, which is the Latin for "draw out"—they bring out the best in us: "They see sparks in their students, have faith in that potential and work toward facilitating and midwifing exponential growth."[9]

Great teachers encourage us to revise our work, rather than accept a grade without grumbling. Honest and forthright, they tell us where and how we can improve, and they offer specific opportunities for doing so. They model vulnerability and creative openness. As a result, students can begin to see themselves more fully—more than egos encased in brains either vying for approval or rejecting social expectations and rebelling. They can begin to loosen their grip on all the myriad ways they attempt to elevate their egos, trying to get what they really want: acceptance, love, to know that they belong in this world, to know that they're OK.

LETTING GO

Although we may practice intentionally leaving our egos at the door, sometimes it takes a big fire to burn out parts of ourselves that continue to create an inflated sense of self as better than others. When the fire burns through, we want to hold onto whatever we can. Yet when there is a fire, new growth becomes possible. A wildfire fire burned out some of Janine's ego a few years ago. She had been teaching graduate seminars nearly every semester since 2005 and had never had a student drop the class after the semester began. However, in fall 2014 five sociology students dropped Janine's Environmental Sociology graduate seminar after the initial class meeting.

At first Janine's mind grasped onto excuses (sociology graduate offerings were slim; students were only taking the class because it was offered; they weren't the right fit anyway). Next, her mind jumped to self-condemnation (I'm not a real sociologist; I'm an imposter; the students see through my act). Two of the students who dropped would not even look in Janine's direction when she passed them in the hall. She didn't know what to do. Should she talk with them? Should she pretend like nothing happened? Should she ask them why they dropped? The fire sizzled throughout the semester and wiped out some part of Janine that thought she owned these courses.

Until then she had not realized how much her ego was bound up with the success of these classes. It was only when this success was challenged that Janine realized how she had attached her sense of self to them. In success she felt a sense of self-worth, and in failure she felt defeated.

From this scorched ground grew a humbler teacher—one who appreciates the students who choose to take a class with her and one who no longer identifies the class as "mine." While she never fully understood why so many students dropped the course that semester, through reflecting on her own teaching approaches, she realized that she often assigned books that inspired her but did not consider materials that might be most relevant to students' particular course of study. Furthermore, she assumed that she knew what graduate students needed to learn and had not taken student feedback about what and how they wanted to learn as seriously as she once had.

Janine entered the next semester with a new sensibility, with a new orientation grounded in gratitude for having opportunities to co-learn with a group of dedicated students. Working with students has taken on a more collaborative quality and connecting with students continues to unfold and enables Janine to better support them in learning.

In the wake of a forest fire the land takes some time to recover. During that period the land rests. Slowly, seeds take root, wild grasses sprout up, and eventually wildflowers color the landscape. As we leave our egos at the door, whether intentionally through reflexive or contemplative practices or unintentionally as when fires burn through, new patterns of being and behaving in the world are born.

We conclude this chapter with a teacher's journal entry:[10]

Over the past few years greater numbers of students have been appearing in my classes with serious and sometimes life-threatening illnesses. They amaze me with their commitment to pursue their education, even while moving in and out of hospitals, dragging themselves to class emaciated, with sores on their bodies, dark eyes dropping deeply into their eye sockets. They struggle. We struggle together.

When discussing aging in America, Holly shares with the class that young people facing death also similarly experience some of the challenges faced by elders in our society. Holly may not live past this semester. I drop my agenda. I listen to the truth of Holly's words and let them penetrate. I take a deep breath, and share that I resonate with what she has shared. Facing our mortality is not easy, and for me, facing my child's cancer diagnosis had not been easy.

As I share this with the class, a moment of vulnerability seems to pass between Holly and me, witnessed by the rest of the students. We continue to discuss aging in America. Yet, for a moment, nothing seems to exist except our shared humanity, our presence. No teacher, no student, no defenses, no egos. To me, this is teaching with compassion.

This is touching

QUESTIONS FOR FURTHER REFLECTION

1. What memories do you have of a teacher who taught with an inflated ego?
2. What memories do you have of a teacher who left her or his ego at the door? How did this person exhibit teaching from a place of humility and vulnerability?
3. In what way have you blamed students for problems that arise in the classroom or for shortcomings in their work? How might you shift the blame and assume some accountability for these issues?
4. What are your greatest limitations as a teacher? What do you do to compensate for or cover up your vulnerabilities, limitations, and flaws? What would it look like to radically accept these limitations?
5. Get creative! Freewrite and create a story that begins as follows: *As I left my ego at the door . . .*

Chapter Five

Focus on Classroom Chemistry

I aim to cultivate a cohesive community of learners in order to foster a humanizing educational experience.

Peter first met Vlad when he showed up in an Introduction to Sociology class. He made quite a first impression: covered in tattoos and body piercings, with a classic surfer's head of hair dyed blue. Before walking into Peter's class, Vlad had made stops at other colleges and had sampled many majors. He just could not quite figure out what he wanted to study and what he wanted to do. Ultimately, Vlad found a home in sociology. But just as important, Peter found something, too.

After that initial introductory class, Vlad went on to take five other classes with Peter, including one where he served as a teaching assistant. It didn't escape Peter's attention that whether Vlad was participating as a student or teaching assistant, the classes where he showed up always had great chemistry. He was the type of student who put others at ease, who broke the ice, who set the right tone, and who led by example.

Vlad was never the most talkative student in class but he was always fully present in the classroom—listening carefully to others, demonstrating respect by everything he said and did, acting in an inclusive and accommodating manner, and doing his part to make the classroom feel like a true community. During the years that Vlad was in Peter's classes, Peter learned a lot about what it takes to cultivate that mysterious thing called classroom chemistry.

As any educator knows, classroom chemistry is an elusive element that is sometimes difficult to socially engineer. It may materialize in one class and totally evaporate in the next. This is not to suggest that we do not have *any* control over fostering it; however, our powers of influence may be more limited than we may want to admit. Nevertheless, if we want to foster a humanizing educational experience, then the atmosphere of the learning environment is critical.

So, what is meant by *classroom chemistry*?

Much like the chemical elements of the Periodic Table, which work together to create all living and natural things of the world, the chemistry between members of a classroom works together to create the educational experience. Sometimes the chemistry is in a state of balance resulting in a high-functioning, energetic, and comfortable classroom, and sometimes it is in a state of imbalance resulting in varying states of dysfunction and disarray.

Absent of having a student like Vlad at our disposal, the question becomes how to cultivate classroom chemistry. How do we bring the many different individual elements in our class into a harmonious, mutually supportive, and connected whole? What specific aspects of the classroom composition and structure should we be especially attentive to? And how does this classroom chemistry contribute to a humanizing and compassionate educational experience?

Equally important, we must consider what happens when our best efforts, our most creative activities, and our unbridled enthusiasm are not enough to produce the winning formula. We must be able to adapt to those classes that clearly lack chemistry despite our best teaching tools and strategies. Instead of blaming the students because the class is not transpiring the way *we* want it to be, we may learn from these challenging experiences and feel energized to be more successful next time.

Even though classroom chemistry is sometimes exceedingly hard to generate, it is still well worth the effort.

THE STATUE OF LIBERTY CLASSROOM:
WELCOMING TO ALL

> Give me your tired, your poor,
> Your huddled masses yearning to breathe free,
> The wretched refuse of your teeming shore.
> Send these, the homeless, tempest-tost to me,
> I lift my lamp beside the golden door!

You may recognize these famous words from Emma Lazarus's sonnet "New Colossus," which adorns the pedestal of the Statue of Liberty. These words, and Lady Liberty herself, suggest what it takes to create a welcoming classroom. Just as the Statue of Liberty invites unfettered and nondiscriminating acceptance of all who seek entrance to our shores, so too might we fashion our classrooms as inviting entry points full of acceptance, warmth, and kindness.

Creating this Statue of Liberty classroom requires attention to the individuals in the class, the physical space in which the class exists, and of course, our own actions in response to these first two points. In effect, these three components are interrelated. If we want to fashion a cohesive, and subsequently compassionate, classroom, then we need to focus on the people, the place, and the teaching process to produce an environment that students find cohesive and compassionate.

Being mindful of who is in our classes is arguably the most important element of classroom chemistry. After having Vlad in a few classes, and seeing how those classes transpired, Peter felt more confident about the possibility of nurturing classroom chemistry in the subsequent classes that Vlad took with him. But even with Vlad around, Peter did not neglect the importance of building relationships with and among all of the members of the class.

This begins with the simple act of learning students' names, a challenge for those teaching in large lecture halls or for high school teachers with upwards of a hundred students (or more), but the classroom experience is greatly humanized when teachers make the effort perhaps simply by learning the names of five or ten students each day.

To be a good host, it is also necessary to spend some time ensuring that students build relationships among themselves. Just because students take classes together doesn't mean they automatically know each other. Even students in high school, who may have had years of schooling together, may be in a class where they are comfortable with only a select few individuals.

Emphasizing the importance of everyone in the class knowing each other, and then taking some time each day to allow this to happen—maybe by asking students at the beginning of each class session to chat with someone they don't know, learn something new, and report back—is the most basic and important component of fostering classroom chemistry.

This may not always be met with enthusiasm. As MIT professor Sherry Turkle points out in her aptly titled book *Alone Together*, today's students may not value or feel comfortable with face-to-face connections.[1] Some even may not place a high premium on making lasting, in-person connections with classmates and they may even view such efforts as an intrusive burden.

Students may be far more comfortable interacting on social media and staying in their "friend bubbles" than meeting and learning about each other in the classroom. Such challenges notwithstanding, the importance of being able to create a classroom where students and teachers talk with each other as real people, knowing their likes and dislikes, cannot be overstated.

Of course, to ensure that students feel the kind of welcome that will enable them to engage with each other, with us, and with the material, we need to understand and accommodate any concerns they may have, any educational troubles they may have experienced, or any areas in which they may appreciate additional assistance. Students are often understandably reluctant to approach a new teacher with information that highlights weakness or potential problems.

For this reason, it is our job to go above and beyond. It isn't enough to mention in passing that students with special concerns need to see you privately. We recommend taking the time to discuss the purpose of communicating such concerns and the format for doing so, perhaps even adding any stories or examples about the kinds of issues you can help with. In other words, make a big deal about this so that students know you are serious, that it's clear to them that you really do care about them. As we have noted many times throughout this book, it is all too easy to make assumptions about students, assumptions that can undermine engagement, learning, and that all-too-elusive classroom chemistry. A case in point follows.

Peter had volunteered to teach a four-week lifetime learning class for senior citizens. On the second day of class, he planned to have the class participate in a mini version of a silent discussion writing exercise that he does with college classes (see two versions of this exercise in chapter 6, "Listen with Intention").[2] In this exercise, students write their responses to an initial prompt that asks them to share their views on an important issue and then read the responses of other students and write subsequent responses to them.

Peter uses this exercise to purposely try to cultivate a welcoming classroom atmosphere by not putting anyone on the spot to speak in front of the whole class about a topic that might be somewhat sensitive or charged. Assuming that this exercise would transpire much like it does in his college classes, he jumped in without checking in with students about engaging in an activity that depended on in-class writing.

If Peter had checked in, he might have found out that two of these senior citizens had arthritis and one had early-onset Parkinson's disease. All three had difficulty writing—as he eventually found out when he was barely able to decipher their responses. They all gamely persevered through the exercise and did not even complain about it, but it was not the most welcoming way to begin a new class.

Welcoming students means welcoming the whole student—especially by embracing their cultural identities, histories, and heritages. Educator and researcher Donna Ford explains:

When teachers are culturally responsive, they are student centered; they eliminate barriers to learning and achievement and, thereby, open doors for culturally different students to reach their potential. In other words, to be culturally responsive means that teachers proactively and assertively work to understand, respect, and meet the needs of students who come from cultural backgrounds different from their own.[3]

We can create culturally responsive classrooms by observing cultural difference and incorporating our observations into culturally responsive curriculum, instruction, and assessment. We might ask ourselves, what are the visual cues that create a welcoming environment for all students from all backgrounds? What materials can be incorporated in the curriculum to address multiple perspectives, voices, and backgrounds? What changes in teaching style can be made in order to respond to multiple ways of learning? How can tests be altered to decrease cultural bias?

We do need to be careful, however, that our good intentions do not go awry. As educator Donna Deyhle points out, it is important to be critically reflective of our own efforts to create an inclusive and welcoming space. Speaking specifically about the typical depiction of Native Americans on K–12 classroom posters, she cautions educators to be aware of the image that is being conveyed especially when we are trying to "counter the all-too-typical lack of images of nonwhite peoples." She offers the following set of helpful questions to guide our decisions:

> Is the image frozen in time, rather than appropriately labeled as a historical image? Is it used as a generic portrait of a "group," rather than as a portrait of some members of that group? Is it a portrait that misrepresents group members' real lives in the contemporary world? Does it present students with limited choices of possible selves? Will students "see" themselves with pride or shame when they look at the poster?[4]

It is unrealistic to think that we can be attuned to every dimension of who students are, what they bring to the classroom in terms of limitations and special needs, and how their backgrounds and upbringings shape their educational experiences. But even if there are gaps in how much we know about students, we can still make a pledge to ourselves that we will be genuinely open to learning about them, honoring who they are as individuals, and welcoming them wholeheartedly into the community of learners. Taking such steps fosters an inclusive classroom environment and conveys our care and concern for each student's experience.

EXERCISE: CREATING A WELCOMING CHECKLIST

The effort to make students feel welcome may easily get lost in the chaotic busyness of being a teacher. This is where a Welcoming Checklist comes in. Many of us depend on checklists for any number of important tasks and responsibilities. Welcoming students is no exception.

Creating this checklist can be done alone or as a brainstorming exercise with colleagues. Some grade levels, departments, or entire schools may want to create their own collective version as a way for all teachers to be attentive and attuned to this dimension of teaching with compassion. The checklist can also be a living document to the extent that items can be added to it as the need arises. Students may even be invited to help craft the checklist and add items to it.

As you begin the task of crafting your Welcoming Checklist, it might be helpful to focus specifically on people, place, and process: how you welcome students, how you create a welcoming space, and how you engage in teaching practices that foster a welcoming experience and environment.

The following items are a few basic suggestions to help get the process started.

- Make an effort to learn a few names each day. Learn all students' names by [date].
- Learn something personal about students (hobbies, favorite foods, pets they may have, where they grew up, goals and aspirations, etc.) by [date]. In the first two weeks do at least two activities that will help students get to know one another.
- Encourage students to tell me about any concerns they may have, educational troubles they may have experienced, or areas in which they may appreciate additional assistance.
- Tell the students something about myself (hobbies, favorite foods, pets I have, where I grew up, etc.).
- Facilitate regular and ongoing opportunities for students to get to know and respect each other throughout the semester. (An example would be using silent discussion to promote engagement and understanding.)
- Do a mirror check periodically in an attempt to detect any unintentional biases or stereotypes that I may be invoking.

THE PHYSICS OF CLASSROOM CHEMISTRY

We also create classroom chemistry through the ways we organize physical space. As many elementary teachers know well, crafting classroom space is an art form in and of itself. Whether it is the kindergarten teacher who carefully arranges the bookshelves, student desks, and learning tables; the science teacher who creates an alluring laboratory full of manipulatives and possibilities; or the special area teacher who goes to great lengths to create an inviting and unique atmosphere that conveys to students the joy of music, art, or physical education, the way in which we set up the learning space says a lot about how we want the educational experience to transpire.

In short, the sensitivity and effort taken to shape classroom space highlights the intentions behind our teaching. And whether those intentions are to ignite and foster a spirit of adventure, optimize skill development, or create a nurturing environment, the care and attention placed in our organization and use of space help us create thriving learning environments where student interactions with the material and with each other can result in great chemistry.[5]

Even when the material is largely abstract and structural limitations exist, as it is in many college classrooms, we can use space creatively. For instance, in her Introductory Sociology class, which often has over a hundred students and is held in lecture halls with immovable tables and chairs, Janine stages simulations in the aisles, uses the corners of the room and hallways to conduct small group work, and hustles around from group to group encouraging student engagement. She refuses to allow the class size or the room constraints to result in an impersonal and isolating educational experience.

In smaller seminars she uses the entire campus as her classroom, engaging students in walk-and-talks both within and outside of buildings. The graduate student who taught Janine this technique explained, "When we walk and talk, sometimes we access different parts of our minds and ourselves than when we're sitting still in chairs around a table. You're often able to delve into a conversation with a friend and go a little more deeply when taking a casual stroll together."

The point here is to think creatively about how we may manage or even manipulate the space. We know that as physical structures, many classrooms at all levels and at all institutions are not conducive to creating a warm, inviting, and communal learning atmosphere. In our commitment to teaching with compassion, overcoming these structural impediments is often one of our greatest challenges.

The following exercise, creating a Learning Café, is one way to possibly surmount some of the physical limitations to create lasting classroom chemistry.

The objective of the exercise is to honor all student perspectives and create an environment where all voices are heard. Learning Cafés engage students in connecting with their own experiences and diverse ways of knowing and thinking. As facilitators of the Learning Café, teachers have the opportunity to take a step back from being the "sage on the stage" and instead practice deep listening.

---

 festina

EXERCISE: LEARNING CAFÉ

The beauty of the Learning Café is that it can be adapted to any topic, subject matter, or even grade level. It is not too early to engage students in kindergarten and the early grades in respectful listening and speaking.

To begin a Learning Café, it is helpful to first engage students in a discussion about deep listening and respect for difference. Depending on the grade level you might also want to outline specific guidelines. But for all ages you want to begin by emphasizing that the purpose of the activity is to learn how to listen. Here are some sample prompts to begin the exercise:

For secondary and college-age students: *Today, you will have an opportunity to share thoughts, ideas, and feelings with your classmates in an atmosphere of nonjudgmental acceptance and appreciation of differing perspectives. When engaging in deep listening with each other we suspend certainty and truly encounter each other, responding and sharing in ways that maintain open exploration and enable us to build ideas and insights together.*

For elementary students: *Today, we are doing something exciting. We will be learning about sharing and listening. Before we get started let's talk about listening.*

Here are some questions designed to engage students in a discussion of what deep listening is.

1. When in your life have you felt deeply listened to? How did you feel when you felt someone was deeply listening to you? How did you know this person was listening? Note: For younger students you may want to begin with an example, perhaps from your own life. Here is a model: *I remember when my father used to listen to my stories about _____. I could tell he was listening because he always asked me questions and wanted more details. He never interrupted me and waited patiently while I spoke. It made me feel like he really cared and like I was important.*

2. How have you practiced deeply listening to another person? How does it feel to practice deep listening?
3. Have you ever encountered someone whose ideas were radically different from your own? Were you able to listen to those ideas or did you jump in with your own ideas? What would it take to truly listen to someone whose ideas diverge from your own ideas? Note: Most young students can engage this question with small adjustments to the vocabulary.

After discussing deep listening, assign students to groups of four to six students. Provide each group with a package of colored markers and a large sheet of paper (giant table-sized Post-it notes are very useful for this exercise). Pass out a handout (an example follows) with clearly outlined directions—this can be adjusted in age-appropriate ways or eliminated altogether. Entitle the handout based on the lesson for that particular class period. You will also need to have a "talking piece"—a symbolic item that designates who has the attention of the class.

EXAMPLE HANDOUT

Café Style Learning[6]

1. Choose a host for your table. This person will be responsible for conveying the ideas of your group to another group of people.
2. Together, explore the following question: [insert your question here]
   Examples:
   For third grade students: How would you change the world if you could?
   For an earth science class: How may we create just and sustainable communities?
   For teachers: What type of compassion practices will best support our pedagogical goals?
3. Share. One person begins by picking up the talking piece and sharing her or his response to the question. After sharing please pass the talking piece to the person to the left. When you receive the talking piece, you may share something or silently pass the talking piece to the next person. Remember: silence carries as much importance as words.
4. Actively listen. Please actively listen while another is talking. Be spontaneous with your own responses (not planning what you will say while others are talking). Active listening can also involve taking notes on the large sheets in front of you, but the notes don't always have to be words. As you listen to others you may draw what you hear in the form of images

and words. These table notes serve as a collective memory of the conversation and will help us identify patterns and connections among ideas. So please write and draw!

5. Shift seats. After fifteen minutes, everyone except for the host moves tables.
6. During this second round you have an opportunity to cross-pollinate ideas. The host shares some of the insights developed by the previous group, and members can each share one insight that arose from their previous group. Then this new group continues building on the conversation.

After fifteen minutes, the teacher rings a bell or somehow indicates that it is time to shift seats. Again, everyone except for the host moves to other tables. The host shares with the new group a summary of the previous group's ideas, and the new group continues to build on these ideas. After three to four rounds, the teacher brings the class together to harvest and share collective discoveries. Every student can take a moment to write down a key insight from the conversations in which they participated.

Next, table hosts post their large paper (now filled with collective insights into the question raised) on a wall in the front of the room and walk the full class through the doodles, thoughts, and conversations shared among the many students who circulated by that table. Individuals can add to these conversations, patterns can be identified (by both students and teacher), and the teacher can note key collective insights that have arisen. Students can go around the room sharing the one insight they wrote down, further building on the insights of each group. As students share and cross-pollinate ideas, they listen and learn from each other, expanding their understanding beyond their own individual understanding.

By using talking pieces and encouraging multiple ways of knowing and forms of expression (e.g., coloring, writing, talking, listening), students are welcomed into an open environment of respect and exploration. The teacher takes on the role of a facilitator, drawing out and gathering both collective insights and the wisdom of each student. Every student has an opportunity to share as others listen. Multiple ways of learning are encouraged, including learning through dialogue, listening, writing, drawing, interpretation, and analysis of patterns.

BALANCING THE SCALES OF EQUITY AND JUSTICE

The more equal social conditions become, the more do [people] display this reciprocal disposition to oblige each other.

—Alexis de Tocqueville, *Democracy in America*[7]

It is impossible to cultivate classroom chemistry if some students feel singled out, disregarded, or treated differently based on who they are. And yet, as longtime educator Pedro Noguera reminds us, it is well established that the majority of students who receive disciplinary punishment in K–12 schools are "students who have learning disabilities, are from single-parent households, are in foster care, are homeless, or qualify for free or reduced-price lunch. In many schools, these students are disproportionately students of color."[8]

This process of singling students out is often referred to as spotlighting. If done judiciously and sensitively, spotlighting can contribute to creating classroom cohesion by highlighting the positive contributions and qualities of students who may otherwise be reticent or reluctant to share. Sometimes, however, spotlighting can be done in a negative and disrespectful manner. The most common forms of negative spotlighting reflect the punitive practices that Noguera mentions earlier.

Another form of troublesome spotlighting may occur when students are signaled out to inform the rest of the class about their race, ethnicity, culture, or religious practices. Even if the intention here is to positively highlight and affirm the students' background, the unintentional effect may be adverse. The attention thrust upon the student may be "reductive, or simply unwanted [and it] creates physical and psychological discomfort that limits students' engagement in the learning process."[9]

It bears emphasizing that spotlighting often presents itself as a racial phenomenon; students of color are disproportionately spotlighted at all levels of education. If we are serious about creating classroom chemistry we must be willing to acknowledge this trend as well as the fact that racism at the individual and institutional level is still deeply entrenched in the fabric of society. Committing ourselves to being antiracist educators and striving to create equitable, just, and antiracist classrooms are prerequisites to fostering classroom chemistry.[10]

To this end, it is important that we are reflective about how students' experiences in the classroom may be interpreted through a very different lens than one's own.[11] For example, in talking about how to create safe spaces in predominantly white classrooms, sociologist Pamela Perry points out that "interactions that feel ordinary and harmless to [white educators] can be experienced by students of color as exclusionary and ostracizing. Even the most committed antiracist educators can unwittingly provoke such responses."[12]

Perry continues,

> White teachers and white students are often oblivious to the painful and alien-ating effects that white-dominated classrooms can have on students of color. Classes can be white-dominated numerically, culturally, and/or socially; yet to white people in those spaces, the norms that regulate the space can feel normal and neutral rather than race-specific. White teachers in predominantly white classrooms must thus stay open to the feedback for students of color in order to learn when our behaviors unintentionally make them feel afraid.[13]

In trying to teach with compassion and build a cohesive classroom environ-ment that reflects this goal, educators must work to eradicate these felt and perceived threats, dangers, and harms. No students should feel estranged from the learning process. All students must know that their voices are heard, their presence is appreciated, their insights are incorporated, their hopes and dreams are encouraged, and their fears are acknowledged.

A TRUE COMMUNITY OF LEARNERS

In trying to bring about cohesive chemistry we acknowledge that the class-room is a community of learners; it is not just a random assemblage of disparate individuals who happen to show up at the same time and place every week. *Community* is an important word here. When we speak about community we are talking about people who are looking out for each other, who are committed to the common good, and who feel a mutual level of trust and respect with one another. Community, much like the word *chemistry*, can connote sympathy and compassion.

Feminist educator bell hooks points out in *Teaching to Transgress* that a cohesive classroom is one where everyone feels as if they bring something to the classroom, where there is a shared "responsibility to contribute." As educators, we can set the tone and model what such a learning environment looks like: "I enter the classroom with the assumption that we must build 'community' in order to create a climate of openness and intellectual rigor. . . . It has been my experience that one way to build community in the class-room is to recognize the value of each individual voice."[14]

More than anything else, community suggests, indeed necessitates, in-terdependence. In all communities, people rely on each other to get things done. Whether it is accomplishing shared goals, supporting and sustaining each other, or even challenging each other to do and be better, communities that thrive are all characterized by people who recognize their reliance on others.

Karen Armstrong points out that compassion is "born of our deep interdependence" with one another and is "essential to human relationship and to a fulfilled humanity."[15] This point is echoed by the philosopher Martha Nussbaum who, in her essay about compassion being the basic social emotion, argues that: "Compassion is a central bridge between the individual and the community; it is conceived of as our species' way of hooking the interests of others to our own personal goods."[16]

Despite these assertions, there is an ethos in Western culture that is even more pronounced than interdependence: individualism. This attitude is on full display in most educational institutions with the focus on high-stakes competition, the culture of individual awards and accolades, and even the predilection for blaming individual students for their shortcomings instead of looking at the external forces that are contributing, if not causing, their maladaptive behaviors.

Overcoming this tilt toward the individual—what Marc Barasch refers to in *The Compassionate Life* as the "I-Me-Mine mentality"—and shifting the focus to the collective is no simple task. But if we want the classroom to be a supportive and safe space of openness, camaraderie, and reciprocity, then we will need to prioritize an interdependent community of learners. Just as students need to feel welcomed and accepted, and just as they need to feel as if they are being treated fairly and justly, so too do they need to feel as if they are invaluable cogs in the wheels of learning.

But in recognizing the interdependent nature of the classroom, we cannot lose sight of the fact that the goal is cohesion of individuals, not conformity of minds. A compassionate classroom is not one where everyone is expected to agree. Nor is it one where everyone is even expected to be best friends. However, it is a space that promotes mutual respect and appreciation for the contributions that others make to the classroom. All students walk through our doors each day with a wealth of experiential wisdom. A classroom environment fashioned on interdependence and community building relishes this widespread wisdom and mines it for the benefit of all.

We end this chapter with one of our favorite exercises for teaching with compassion and for creating classroom chemistry. This exercise touches on many of the themes of this chapter. It strengthens bonds among students, it scaffolds in such a way that it builds an interdependent community, and it fosters empathy by having students learn about each other beyond the surface level.

EXERCISE: THE SIMILARITIES PROJECT

The Similarities Project[17] grew out of the sociological insight that our differences are often emphasized and exacerbated to create divisions and boundaries. We construct artificial and arbitrary distinctions between me and you, us and them. Then, we use these distinctions to connect exclusively with others like us. These separations can quickly become solidified, making it difficult to cultivate a cohesive classroom community.

The Similarities Project was crafted to break down these divisions and demonstrate to students that we have many more commonalities that align us and potentially push us together than differences that may pull us apart. Despite prevailing beliefs to the contrary, all humans are much more similar than they are different. This exercise goes a long way in demonstrating this point and building stronger and lasting connections among members of the class.

The exercise can be done with a single class, with two classes, or even with an entire grade level or school. Janine has had success doing this exercise with a class of sixty students and Peter often brings one of his sociology classes to a local elementary school to do the exercise with elementary school children and college students.

Step 1. Arrange the class into groups of two and ask these pairs to find ten things that they have in common. They can identify anything they want as long as they both have the answers in common.

Step 2. Combine two pairs together so that there are now multiple groups of four students. Remind the members of the group to introduce themselves to each other. Ask these new groups of four to compare their lists, cross off the items that all four do not share, circle the answers they do share, and find ten more new things that all four of them have in common.

Step 3. Combine the groups of four into groups of eight. Remind the members of the group to introduce themselves to each other. Ask these new groups of eight to compare their lists, cross off the items that all eight of them do not share, circle the answers they do share, and find ten more new things that all eight of them have in common.

Steps 4, 5, 6, etc.: Continue this process of joining groups together until the class is back together as a whole. In the final stage, create a master list of all of the things that everyone in the room has in common.

The Similarities Project gets increasingly difficult after each step of the exercise. It is common for some groups to be stuck on finding ten items that they all have in common. Sometimes, in the interest of time, it may be necessary to move onto the next step before all of the groups have come up with a new list of ten items. Moving the exercise along in this fashion is not a problem in order to leave enough time to have the group back together as a whole.

After the whole group is reconvened, it is useful to make a list of the responses for everyone to view and discuss. The class can then discuss how these similarities compare to the many differences that society emphasizes and exaggerates as we create divisions among us. In some classes, it may be appropriate to give students paper and crayons and ask them to illustrate one of the similarities from the list.

The overall point to convey is that similarities are more tangible, more lasting, and more significant than the socially created differences that we too often accentuate. To drive this point home further, you can add some of the following similarities to the master list if they were not already mentioned. The items on this list emphasize our basic humanness and common humanity:

good list!

We all like to laugh.
We all experience happiness.
We all experience sadness.
We will all experience failure.
We all experience disappointment.
We all have people we love.
We all have people who love us.
We all have friends.
We all have people we dislike.
We all have people who dislike us.
We all have prejudices and biases.
We all have stereotypes.
We all need social interaction to feel human.
We all need clean air to breathe.
We all need potable water.
We all need arable land.
We all must eat to live.
We all need shelter.
We all live on planet Earth.
We all need the energy of the sun.
We all need natural resources.
We all must coexist with other species.

We all rely on other living organisms (plants, animals, and insects) to survive.
We are all affected by gravity.
We are all affected by the environment.
We are all humans.
We all have a beating heart.
We all are comprised of cells.
We all have virtually the same DNA (99.9 percent).
We all communicate verbally or nonverbally.
We all need to sleep.
We all need to pee and poop.
We all bleed.
We are all affected by technology.
We all live in a country.
We all suffer from war.
We all have ancestors.
We were all born to a mother.
We all have names.
We all have a family.
We are all assigned a gender.

We are all assigned a race/ethnicity.   We all have dreams and aspirations.
We are all assigned a nationality.   We will all eventually die.
We all have values.

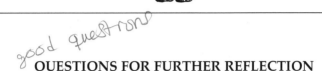

QUESTIONS FOR FURTHER REFLECTION

1. Have you ever had a student like Vlad whose mere presence seemed to greatly assist in fostering classroom chemistry? What was it about this student that helped create a stronger learning environment?

2. Have you ever had an anti-Vlad—in other words, a student whose actions challenged the cohesion of the classroom? What steps did you take to address this situation? What lessons did you learn from this student that might help you build classroom cohesion in the future?

3. If you could create the ideal classroom space to teach with compassion, what would it look like? Assuming it is not possible to fully realize this ideal, are there components of it that you could incorporate despite the physical and structural limitations you face?

4. In addition to race and ethnicity, what other aspects of a student's identity are commonly associated with an unjust, unfair, and unequal classroom experience? How might we be sensitive to these other variables so as to mitigate their potentially harmful effect on classroom cohesion?

5. In what ways do your current teaching practices promote individualism and competition? How might these practices be revamped so that they promote interdependence and cooperation?

Chapter Six

Listen with Intention

I listen deeply, wholly, and actively to students by taking in their words, gestures, and silence.

Imagine this: You are in front of your class, presenting a lesson that you labored over when you notice that many of the students seem restless and inattentive. You offer a friendly nudge, "This is important; you all need to pay close attention." But after a few moments, the restlessness returns. A few more friendly nudges and prods, and your frustration level rises until you lose it entirely, calling out, "You all are not listening to me. C'mon now, let's pay attention!"

But what if, at that moment, instead of rousing themselves again, the students replied in unison: "You are not listening *to us!*"

Our confidence in our own communication skills and our zeal to convey the material may make it difficult for us to receive the full meaning of the messages students send us via their quizzical looks, furrowed brows, starry eyes, head scratches, and slumping bodies. We may not even hear the deep levels of confusion behind the timid questions they ask or the embarrassed "uh-huh" they offer when we ask if they are with us.

Listening is not just about hearing sounds. It is the act of being fully present with what arises in any particular moment. If students appear disengaged or seem to not be listening, how can we be present with them and listen to their disengagement? How may we become cognizant of the more nuanced messages that students may be conveying? How do we become aware of not only their words but also the experiences, thoughts, feelings, and emotions that are behind these words?

In this chapter, we explore what it means to listen with intention. We view teaching with compassion as an activity purposefully devoted to deep listening so that we become more attentive to students' experiences. Deep listening goes beyond just listening to the utterances of words. It entails strengthening our skills of perception so that we may read body language and nonverbal gestures, respect and honor voluntary (and involuntary) silence, and even seek insight into the daily lives of students so that we can more fully comprehend the context of their thoughts.

DEEP LISTENING: HEARING WITH OUR EYES AND SEEING WITH OUR EARS

Deep listening is the process of listening between the words as much as to the content of the words. Deep listening also means paying attention and not planning what you will say while another is speaking. When we listen deeply, we remain both externally silent (we don't speak while another is speaking) and internally silent (we don't get wrapped up in our own thoughts). Finally, deep listening engages the heart as well as the mind. (Please see the exercise in chapter 5, "Focus on Classroom Chemistry," on creating Learning Cafés for ideas on facilitating deep listening in the classroom.)

Zen Buddhists often refer to hearing with our eyes and seeing with our ears. As educators, it is a useful reminder about how we may go beyond words in order to more fully grasp what students are experiencing.

Hearing with Our Eyes

By hearing with our eyes, we take notice of what we see and observe. Hearing with our eyes expands our senses so that we are more fully present in the moment, more attentive to what is happening for students, and more focused on student experiences. When we make an effort to hear with our eyes we do not limit our capacity to listen. In the process of teaching and learning, hearing with our eyes helps us gauge what is happening in the classroom. We may not be able to hear every word or conversation but we can read body language, observe facial reactions, and perceive emotions.

Hearing with our eyes is not limited to the classroom. We may employ this listening skill in conversations with students in our offices or even while walking alone around the school or campus community. Whether through observing signs on bulletin boards, chalking on school walkways, or even the forms of relaxation that students engage in, by using our eyes to hear what students are up to we are better equipped to understand their world and subsequently offer them guidance and support.

In this sense, hearing with our eyes may help us know students more intimately while honoring their need for their own space. From a comfortable distance we may become more familiar with students' experiences today, which are probably quite different than our own experiences as students. Gathering this information does not require that we do an undercover anthropological study (as others have done[1]); instead, it merely requires that we open our eyes and use our powers of perception to hear what student life is like. Having this knowledge will help us better relate to students, particularly when they come to us in need. It will also allow us to teach better and make the material more relevant to their lived experiences.

Consider an example of undergraduate students in a queer theory class who were looking particularly forlorn at the beginning of one class period. When the instructor asked her students what was wrong, out came a torrent of grief as they shared their horror over the torture and killing of an LGBT student that had made national news.

modify / adapt

The teacher made a decision. She put aside her scheduled lesson and turned the classroom into a space where students could write messages, letters, poems, and so forth and post these messages around the room. The rest of the class period was spent reading and listening to each other's stories, fears, and distress. In this way, the teacher provided not only an opportunity for the students to express themselves, but also an opportunity for each to feel listened to.

Deep listening is especially important for students facing great difficulties and for students from a range of cultural and socioeconomic backgrounds. Vicki Zakrzewski, educational director of the Greater Good Science Center, highlights research that shows that students who have teachers who demonstrate understanding and compassion for their hardships exhibit more prosocial behaviors and do better in school.[2] One student remarked that if a teacher doesn't show understanding, he thinks, "Oh, they're giving up on me, so I might as well give up on myself."[3] Furthermore, cultural misunderstandings between teachers and students negatively impact students' lives while teachers who make efforts to understand students' backgrounds are in a better position to support them.

Essentially, hearing with our eyes enables us to tune in to students' needs and demonstrate our interest in their lives. Yet we don't always have the time to observe student life. In this case, Zakrzewski suggests having students complete an interest inventory to learn more about their lives and interests.[4] For example, asking students to list their favorite extracurricular activities or their greatest challenges in school can help teachers not only demonstrate interest in students' lives beyond course expectations, but also enable teachers to hear with their eyes, learning what is important and challenging for students.

Hearing with our eyes is especially necessary when students' pain manifests as silence. In educational settings, student silence is sometimes criticized as a form of passivity, shyness, or disengagement. While it is true that some students exhibit quietness for these reasons, silence can also be a coping mechanism for the trials and tribulations that students experience.

By listening with our eyes, we seek to interpret nonverbal cues in order to gain deeper understanding of students. Yet, while our intentions are to listen deeply, it is important to recognize that the activity of listening with our eyes is an interpretive one and therefore limited. As Zakrzewski writes, "A teacher who actively listens to students is listening for the meaning behind what students are saying, *then checks in with them to make sure they've understood properly.* This affirms students' dignity and helps develop a trusting relationship between teachers and students"[5] (italics added).

While we may not always be able to check in with students, as we have noted elsewhere, we should be mindful of any assumptions we have made about their lives. Hearing with our eyes also requires that we acknowledge our own biases and filters, do our best to enter the diverse worlds of the students, and humbly admit that we can never fully know how they perceive the world nor fully know what their experiences are like.

Seeing with Our Ears

Although educators are not superheroes, sometimes we find ourselves in situations wishing we had superhero powers. One trait that could come in handy is having eyes in the back of our heads, especially while we are trying to manage a large classroom, when students are dispersed in small group or lab work, and certainly while we are writing on the board. While such vision is clearly not possible, we can see with our ears and listen to what is going on beyond our eyesight. Strengthening our skills of perception by focusing on auditory instead of visual signals allows us to be more attentive to what students are experiencing.

One of the interesting things about seeing with our ears is that we expect students to do this all of the time. The dominant form of teaching in the United States is still the traditional lecture where students are expected to sit quietly, listen attentively, and ingest all of the information that is being given to them.

This is especially true in the college classroom, where professors attempting to "see" how much the students have learned generally ask them to regurgitate what they have "heard" during class lecture in the form of tests and quizzes. The same is not expected of teachers. What if we were tested on how well we listen to students?

Seeing with our ears means that we listen intently when others speak about their experiences. Seeing is a primary form of perception, but we cannot perceive others' experiences if we do not also hear them. When someone tells us how they feel, what they have experienced, or what they worry about, we need to hear everything. While their words paint a picture for us there are other auditory clues—tone of voice, speech rhythms—that can leave us with an impression of their state of being.

As we listen to someone, we even use phrases such as, "I see what you mean" or "I see where you are coming from." These phrases do not imply vision in a literal sense; instead, we use them to convey comprehension and maybe even some level of empathy. When we use these phrases what we are really saying is: "I hear what you are saying to me, I am attentive and listening to your story. To the best of my ability, I understand your situation."

To fully see with our ears may also require that we shut our mouths. We often need to suspend our urge to respond in turn and offer our own story. It is a common occurrence for one person to tell a story while another interjects with their similar experience. We may even think that interjecting and sharing our story is a way of empathizing with others. We take what the person is telling us, relate it to our own experience, and then shift the conversation from them to us: "Oh, I'm so sorry to hear what happened to you. The same thing happened to me two years ago . . ." *Narcissism*

In *The Pursuit of Attention*, sociologist Charles Derber refers to these "shift responses" as indications of a type of conversational narcissism that threatens our ability to have mutually sustaining conversations. Arising from a society that often promotes individualism and competition over collectivism and cooperation, shift responses and conversational narcissism are antithetical to being compassionate.[6]

As educators, the urge to shift the conversation back to ourselves and demonstrate our expertise on a particular topic is quite real and tempting. And we often do this to illustrate our understanding of the situation and offer an example that we think may help the students. The challenge for us is to be able to balance when we need to keep our mouths shut and listen, and when we should offer a point of connection for clarification.

Hearing with our eyes and seeing with our ears reminds us that teaching is not meant to be a one-directional activity. Teaching requires that we open our eyes, ears, and hearts to students. Through such forms of deep listening we demonstrate to students that we are willing and eager to see and hear them. They are not just faceless and nameless entries in our grade books. They are living and breathing human beings.

LISTENING TO SILENCE

In *The Elephant in the Room: Silence and Denial in Everyday Life*, Eviatar Zerubavel makes the case that silence is a form of speech, "a profoundly active performance" that we need to listen to carefully. Even in the absence of words or verbal explanations, listening to silence may provide a much-needed glimpse into the inner life of the students.[7]

So how can we learn to become more skillful listeners of silence? First, we can identify our own judgments about silent students and our responses to them. When students are silent, we sometimes unintentionally return their silence with silence. It may be hard to focus our teaching energies on students who seem to be withdrawn or who are not actively participating in the class. We both can recall instances where we inadvertently left the silent students behind because our energies and enthusiasms were being reciprocated by the more vocal and seemingly engaged students. As we surveyed the class during discussion, our gaze may have quickly passed over these silent students or we may have even ignored them completely. Perhaps we assumed silent students are unprepared. Or perhaps we blame ourselves and assume that we have not presented the materials in interesting or engaging ways.

There are multiple reasons why students may not speak. Traditional Native American cultures, for example, value observation as the primary mode of learning. Coming from homes where they "watch then do," traditional Native students value silence above talking.[8] When we interpret students' silence, whether it results from differences in culture or even temperament, to mean they are uninterested, unprepared, or not understanding course material, we do an incredible disservice to those whose learning styles are different from ours or different from the predominant learning modalities taught in mainstream education.

Another reason students may be silent is that many are introverted. Susan Cain cites studies that find that one third to one half of people in the nation are introverts. In *Quiet: The Power of Introverts in a World That Can't Stop Talking*, Cain encourages educators to consider how introverts are treated in the classroom. Do the ways in which we structure our lessons and classroom activities end up hindering the more silent reserved students?

Cain maintains that we live in a society that values the "extroverted ideal"—the gregarious person who stands out in a crowd, who is confident, outgoing, talkative, and friendly. Studies have found that extroverts are perceived as smarter, more attractive, and more interesting. Furthermore, we are more easily swayed by the arguments of charismatic extroverted speakers, even if what they say is undeveloped, misinformed, or misguided. As educators, we must ask ourselves: In what ways might we value the contributions of extroverted students and overlook the learning and communication styles of more introverted students?

Many educators, ourselves included, assume that small-group work provides additional opportunities for the quieter students to participate. Enter any school in the United States (elementary school through college) and it is likely that you will find some classrooms with desks arranged in clusters set up for small-group work.

The hope is that these small-group project-based activities will provide more opportunities for student engagement. And they do, yet Cain observes that the silent students may become even more reticent in such settings. Cain offers the example of Maya, a fifth-grade redhead with glasses, working on a group project focused on the three branches of American government. Her group is the executive branch, and a more outgoing group member has passed around a bag, stating that whoever has the bag gets to talk.

> Maya looks overwhelmed when the bag makes its way to her.
>
> "I agree," she says, handing it like a hot potato to the next person.
>
> The bag circles the table several times. Each time Maya passes it to her neighbor, saying nothing. Finally, the discussion is done. Maya looks troubled. She's embarrassed, I'm guessing, that she hasn't participated.[9]

When Maya does try to chime in she immediately clams up. As with most introverts, she's sensitive to others' cues, and sensing disapproval from the "cool kid" in the group, she lowers her eyes and mumbles something that no one else can hear.

Cain remarks:

> The school environment can be highly unnatural, especially from the perspective of an introverted child who loves to work intensely on projects he cares about, and hang out with one or two friends at a time. In the morning, the door to the bus opens and discharges its occupants in a noisy, jostling mass. Academic classes are dominated by group discussions in which a teacher prods him to speak up. He eats lunch in the cacophonous din of the cafeteria, where he has to jockey for a place at a crowded table. Worst of all, there's little time to think or create. The structure of the day is almost guaranteed to sap his energy rather than stimulate it.[10]

Cain's observations are a reminder that we need to listen with compassion and intention to introverted students. We can't take their silence to mean they aren't learning, but we also can't take it to mean we should leave them alone. Instead, we should read it as a cue that we need to consider how to better tap into their strengths and ways of learning.

Sometimes, however, students are indeed communicating something particular via their silence, as educator and writer Herbert Kohl suggests in his classic essay "I Won't Learn from You." Kohl explains how silence can serve as a form of rebellion against racist and oppressive educational structures.[11] Offering examples of minority students who harness "not-learning" as an active form of resistance to the power structures that disrespect their cultural heritage, families, and values, Kohl concludes that willed not-learning is different from failure. By a process that Martin Luther King Jr. called "creative maladjustment," students use a variety of techniques, including silence, to resist oppression.

Kohl explains that it's not that students don't understand or are unable to learn, it is that they refuse and are unwilling to learn the material. Why? Because by rejecting what school wants to teach them, these students preserve their own integrity—they reject the way they feel the educational system thinks about and treats them. Kohl's example of Rick who sat in silence refusing to learn algebra highlights this use of silence as an act of resistance:

> There were emotional reasons Rick refused to learn algebra, but it's essential to distinguish here between his decision to not-learn algebra and his ability to learn it. Rick could have learned algebra quite easily. There was nothing wrong with his mind, his ability to concentrate, or his ability to deal with abstract ideas. He could read, and did read books he chose. He knew how to do very complex building projects and science projects. He enjoyed playing around with athletic statistics and gambling odds. He just rejected the whole idea of being tested and measured against other students and, though he was forced to attend school, there was no way to force him to learn.[12]

Listening to the silence of those who have been consistently and generationally oppressed requires us to open up to the ways that we, too, have been complicit in oppressive systems of education. Listening to silence built of anger and oppression can challenge us to carefully consider the texts we use, the knowledge we expect students to learn (i.e., are we teaching Native American students about the European "explorers" who "discovered America"?), and how we invite students into conversations about their own educational processes.

ᏩᏯᏮᏜ

EXERCISE: THE SILENT DISCUSSION

A useful listening exercise is called the Silent Discussion. Instead of having students talk out loud about a particular topic, the Silent Discussion uses writing as the medium for students to share their thoughts and questions. We offer two versions of the Silent Discussion here. Both versions are particularly useful for topics that might be sensitive or difficult to discuss out loud in class, such as racism, sexism, or homophobia, or as a way of engaging and valuing the contributions of the introverts in the class. The Silent Discussion provides a safer space for hearing the perspectives and experiences of others without anyone feeling put on the spot.

The following exercises, and ones like them, also honor multiple perspectives and provide opportunities for students to share their diverse experiences. Additionally, offering opportunities for silence within a classroom setting appeals particularly to those students who enjoy and need the time and space for quiet reflection.

Version 1

Beginning with a prompt or question, ask students to freewrite their reaction for eight to ten minutes. Once time is up, ask the students to randomly circulate their papers. Next, each person writes a reaction to the paragraph in front of them. After another eight to ten minutes of freewriting, the papers are circulated randomly again and students then write a reaction to both paragraphs in front of them.

As this process continues for a few rounds, a silent and anonymous conversation evolves. Students get to hear the thoughts of their classmates by reading them on paper and then responding with letters to their classmates instead of words spoken aloud. At the end of the exercise, students get back their own paper (by deciphering their handwriting and what they wrote in the first paragraph) and are given time to read the transcript of the conversation that ensued after their initial reaction.

This version of the Silent Discussion is useful because it helps to avoid the problem that often ensues in discussions whereby participants are so keyed up to talk next that they fail to hear what those preceding them are saying. In the Silent Discussion, each person must sit with the words in front of them, hear what others have said, and consider these words as they prepare their response. There is still the possibility that they may hone in on one particular line or comment in the writings; however, the likelihood that they are listening to what they are reading is greater than if they were in a classroom full of multiple voices vying for the stage.

Version 2

Sociologist Deborah Cohan[13] uses a unique approach to silently share viewpoints on controversial topics. This version of the Silent Discussion enables students to express themselves without constraining what they feel or editing themselves to try to please the teacher or each other. It also provides opportunities for both students and teachers to practice deep listening—hearing alternative viewpoints while refraining from judgment.

1. Pose a controversial question (age appropriate and relevant to the course materials). Examples:
   - Should homework be optional?
   - What's the best way to prevent bullying on the playground?
   - Should children's picture books discuss issues such as racism or homosexuality?
   - Should the United States increase, decrease, or maintain the number of refugees permitted to enter the country?
   - Is it racist for athletic teams to use such names as the Washington Redskins and Atlanta Braves?
2. Discuss the importance of civil discussion. For example, you might preface the exercise with something like: *The point of the Silent Discussion is to create an opportunity for open conversation around a topic that has a range of points of view. Please discuss your point of view in a respectful manner. Please refrain from shaming someone else's point of view, perpetuating stereotypes, name-calling, or spreading misinformation. The point of this activity is for you to share your ideas in a way that raises our collective understanding of the diverse ways of thinking about this topic.*
3. Students write their responses to the question. Provide students the option of remaining anonymous by not writing their names on their papers.
4. The teacher reads each response aloud (being careful to read all papers with the same tone and not reveal their own biases through the inflections of their voice). Alternatively, each student can be given someone else's response and read it aloud.
5. Student reflection. To maintain the silence, students can journal about their observations, feelings, and experiences of listening to the different points of view. Alternatively, students can share their impressions in small groups or as a whole class.

HUMANIZING THE CLASSROOM THROUGH LISTENING

There is nothing more human than the simple act of giving attention to another.

—Charles Derber, *Pursuit of Attention*[14]

Listening is an act of open receptivity. When we open up our ears, we in essence open up our hearts and our minds, bringing our presence and attention to another. By deeply listening to those around us we validate their perspective as well as their knowledge, experience, and wisdom. This is a profoundly humanizing act. Through the act of deep listening, we call attention to the qualities that make us human, such as the ability to reflect, create, express, and experience. As we recognize students' humanity through providing them opportunities to share their perspectives, ideas, and experiences, they feel validated, appreciated, and inspired to learn.[15]

An African American student approached Janine after engaging in an interactive class discussion one day. He said, "You have no idea what it means to me to get to share my ideas in this class. I'm on the football team, and no one has ever cared about what I had to say." Janine was both moved by this expression of gratitude and also saddened by the lack of opportunities this student had to share his perspective and understanding. How may we offer more opportunities for students to share their own perspectives and understanding? Furthermore, what do we need to do to remain receptive and deeply listen to the multiple perspectives and experiences that students share?

Through creating opportunities for students to share from their own knowledge base, understanding, and experience, and through actively listening to their responses, students and teachers co-create rich learning experiences. As Martha Caldwell writes in her article "How to Listen with Compassion in the Classroom," "When students share personal stories in the classroom, teachers help them make connections to the larger world they live in. . . . These connections help them consolidate their insights and expand their worldviews."[16]

The point here is not to transform our classes into talk show–like environments where everyone simply states their differing opinions. Instead, the idea is to create enriching learning environments through welcoming and including students' experiences and perspectives in the classroom. We can invite students to share their perspectives, listen intently to their diverse experiences, and help them connect those perspectives and experiences to both the larger class objectives and to the world around them.

Returning to Karen Armstrong's Charter of Compassion as outlined in the introduction, when we listen with intention we *honor the inviolable sanctity of every single being*. We open up our eyes and ears to the experiences, perspectives, and ways of knowing of each and every student. We listen to students' words, actions, and silences. When we listen with intention, we pay attention, practicing deep listening and ultimately listening to students' hearts.

Paula Underwood, clan mother of the Turtle clan of the Iroquois Nation, explains deep listening as the ability to know people's hearts. Valuing listening as a child, Paula got proficient at repeating what others said to her verbatim. One day an elderly neighbor came by her home wanting to talk and share his stories. Paula listened and repeated the old man's stories back to her dad. "You're getting pretty good at that. *Did you hear his heart?*" her father asked.

Her father explained, "He is very lonely and comes and shares his memories with you again and again because he's asking you to keep him company in his memories." Paula came to realize, "My heart echoed his heart. And when you can listen at that level, then you can hear not only the people. If you really pay attention, you can hear what the Universe is saying."[17]

As we practice hearing hearts we humanize the classroom, creating compassionate spaces where students feel validated, appreciated, and inspired to learn.

QUESTIONS FOR FURTHER REFLECTION

1. How do you practice listening to students? How do you hear with your eyes and see with your ears? What are some recent examples of how you have practiced deep listening?
2. What is one intention that you can set that would help you further develop your listening skills in the classroom? Write this intention down and remind yourself of it before you enter the classroom for the next month (e.g., *I will pause and take one mindful breath after each student talks so that I can take in and process what that student is saying*).
3. What do you do to foster a culturally responsive classroom? What can you do to listen yet deeper to the cultural needs of the students? In what ways could you further develop culturally responsive curriculum, instruction, and assessment?
4. Reflect upon this statement written by Vietnamese Zen master, Thich Nhat Hanh: "We can learn how to generate a powerful and healing silence not only in our families . . . but also in our larger community. If you are a schoolteacher, you should know how to nurture that kind of noble, refreshing silence in your class."[18] What are some ways that you foster silence in the classroom? How might students benefit from more opportunities for silence?
5. Consider an upcoming class lesson. What is one thing that you can do to invite students to share their experiences? What kind of activities or discussion questions can you incorporate to help students connect their experiences to the larger learning objectives of that particular lesson?

Chapter Seven

Hold Space

Knowing that students experience stress and uncertainty, I provide opportunities for feeling, reflection, and expression.

Have you ever had one of those brief encounters with someone where, for just a moment, they offered a type of spacious presence that temporarily relieved you of your burdens? Perhaps it was someone's warm, gentle gaze as they said hello to you just after you received some disturbing news. Maybe it was a friend who listened to you without judgment, comment, or attempts to push you into a problem-solving mode as you vented after a challenging day. Or it could have been a loved one who sat with you in silence and allowed you to quietly have your feelings, think, and reflect without feeling the pressure to talk and explain.

When another person invites us to freely express or even simply and silently experience our feelings in an atmosphere of warmth and kindness the results can be powerful and life changing. Through this process we can find the courage, internal strength, and confidence to explore, take risks, and move through the difficult challenges that are thrown our way.

Leadership coach Heather Plett identifies these moments as "holding space," a capacity she describes as a willingness "to walk alongside another person in whatever journey they're on without judging them, making them feel inadequate, [or] trying to fix them."[1]

Plett became intrigued by the quiet power of holding space when she witnessed it in action as hospice workers cared for her dying mother. She was so

PLETT'S EIGHT TIPS FOR HOLDING SPACE

1. Give people permission to trust their own intuition and wisdom.
2. Give people only as much information as they can handle.
3. Don't take their power away.
4. Keep your own ego out of it.
5. Make them feel safe enough to fail.
6. Give guidance and help with humility and thoughtfulness.
7. Create a container for complex emotions, fear, trauma, and so forth.
8. Allow them to make different decisions and to have different experiences than you would.

moved by the loving environment these workers created around her mother that she outlined eight tips for holding space that can be applied to all life situations.

For teachers, holding space means supporting students in their growth and development, providing gentle guidance when needed, creating safe environments to allow them to make and learn from mistakes, and generating opportunities for students to tap into their own inner wisdom. Through compassion, we hold space for students with present moment awareness and tenderness of heart. We meet them in the midst of their struggles, triumphs, fears, and joys just as they are.

When we hold space, we don't only create containers where complex emotions can live and breathe, but we also establish educational environments where students with diverse learning strengths and challenges can thrive. We offer students ample room so that their experiences may unfold.

What does this space look like in today's classrooms and campuses? How can we hold space for students in ways that nourish them and help them grow? How do we teach in ways that open up space rather than close it down? And how may we create space for students to connect with their own wisdom? Drawing on Plett's tips, we now consider how teachers can open up space for students that will allow them to connect with their own inner wisdom, have the confidence to explore and challenge themselves, and grow as learners.

1. GIVE STUDENTS PERMISSION TO
TRUST THEIR OWN INTUITION AND WISDOM

Trusting students' own intuition and wisdom calls on us to open up our minds and connect with them as human beings. Does trusting the intuition of, say, a second grader differ significantly from trusting that of a graduate student?

While the details may look different, we would argue the challenge is actually quite similar. In both cases, trusting students' wisdom requires that we be willing to transcend the rigid roles prescribed by our separate positions as students and teachers.

Janine learned this lesson recently when one of her master's in sustainable communities students, Chase, approached her about writing a master's thesis on how art can decolonize our minds. Chase wanted to take an unconventional approach to writing her thesis, examining the process of decolonizing her own mind through creating art within a natural setting. Janine's first impulse was to take her student through the traditional process designed to build on thinking of previous scholars, first asking Chase to look at the works of five theorists to see what other scholars said on the matter. To her surprise, a few weeks later, Chase came to Janine's office absolutely distraught, crying, and wondering if she was really cut out for graduate work.

Janine was faced with a difficult choice. As a serious scholar, one bound to uphold the standards of her discipline, she wondered briefly if Chase's initial reaction was correct: maybe she wasn't prepared to complete graduate work. But as a teacher dedicated to supporting students with compassion, she chose to step away from those standards long enough to truly hear Chase out.

Compassion required that Janine listen deeply in order to truly understand and support Chase, and she did. She began to recognize the wisdom guiding Chase's approach. In fact, in that extraordinary session, Janine began to see how letting art into the exploration of how to free our minds from deeply embedded societal expectations that reinforce inequalities could have important implications for Chase's field, creating just and sustainable communities.

As Janine listened deeply and began to recognize the wisdom guiding Chase's approach, she began also recognizing Chase as *her* teacher. The theorists that Janine had asked Chase to read were merely reinforcing the academic rigidity from which Chase was actively trying to liberate herself. In this circumstance, holding space for Chase required that Janine drop some of her teacher expectations and send Chase out into the field to explore and liberate her thinking. "Do it!" Janine said. "Spend three months painting in nature. Record your experiences. Free your mind!"

By challenging herself to hold space for Chase, Janine paved the way for a student to write one of the most inspiring and creative theses Janine had read in fifteen years. Given the opportunity to break free from the traditional academic paradigm, Chase was able to gather fresh insights and realize powerful possibilities. Her work even served as motivation for one of her thesis committee members to write a poem about the wild mind.

Janine's decision to trust the wisdom of an adult in graduate school paid off. But what choices are available to teachers of younger students in K–12 classrooms? We understand that young students may not have the maturity and self-knowledge to detail specific proposals for self-study as Chase did; however, if as teachers we listen carefully we can locate and creatively mine their wisdom.

Every day, students give us feedback about how they might learn better, sometimes through concrete suggestions but often in a backhanded way through complaints and protestations. Yes, it is easy to dismiss these as simply avoiding work. What if instead of pushing back or insisting on compliance we decided to occasionally interrogate our lessons more deeply to see if perhaps students didn't have a point? For example, how do we know if the assignments in the state-approved curriculum are easily completed unless we try them for ourselves?

One third-grade teacher we heard from describes just this experience. The district writing curriculum for third grade called for students to write an essay describing their neighborhood. The thinking seemed to be that the essay allowed students to write what they know well, but students didn't see it this way. The minute the teacher gave the assignment students' hands shot up. "I don't have a neighborhood!" said one student. "I don't know what to say," said another. "My neighborhood is no big deal."

That last complaint hit home. The teacher realized that students, just like all of us, wanted to write something special and trying to make something ordinary like a neighborhood into something special was a sophisticated writing problem that they weren't prepared for. So the teacher went back to the drawing board and developed her own prompt, one based on a book that she had been reading to the class that she knew they had found exciting. The next day, when she gave the new prompt, student hands again went up. But this time after asking a few questions for clarification, they quickly dove into the work.

This experience didn't just result in better essays and more student engagement, it provided an important experience for the students, helping them know that they can trust their own responses and also trust the teacher to listen to them. This doesn't mean that every time a student protests a teacher must jump and make changes. The craft of teaching requires that we cultivate our own instincts, learning when to challenge ourselves and push out of our own comfort zones, when to let students take the lead, and when to push against the authority of the disciplines we teach or the institutions we work within.

One of the difficulties of teaching with compassion and realizing this first step of holding space is to allow ourselves to break free from the rigidity and orthodoxy of our teaching practices. As Chase concludes in her thesis, "We humans are animals, not machines, and we do best when we are able to be free with our ideas, conceptions of reality, and impressions of the future. Free of judgment, free of control, and free of limitations. . . . The wild is freedom, and it lies within each and every one of us as humans on this Earth."[2]

2. GIVE STUDENTS ONLY AS MUCH
INFORMATION AS THEY CAN HANDLE

This tip serves as a useful reminder that we should strive to emphasize quality and not overwhelm students with quantity. Holding space for students also means recognizing that there are limitations on what they can and should be forced to absorb. But recognizing and acting on this reality can be especially tricky because many of us who go into education were the type of students who loved learning as much material as possible. We may operate on the assumption that the way to academic excellence is studying for countless hours, burning the wick at both ends, and consuming enormous amounts of information. As a result, we may sincerely believe that maintaining high expectations means assigning a lot of work.

But are these assumptions correct? The research says no. While high expectations are in fact crucial for student success,[3] the strategy of asking students to learn more and learn faster can often backfire, leaving students with no choice but to adopt a model of cramming, memorizing, and regurgitating.

As cognitive researcher and head of the Learning and Forgetting Lab at UCLA Robert Bjork has discovered, this approach does not bring about true learning; instead, it often results in the mere forgetting of the material students tried so hard to retain.[4]

In thinking about how to implement this step, given the institutional constraints we face—whether we are kindergarten teachers charged with teaching reading to many students who may not be ready or college professors challenged to drag our freshmen through the intricate details of an introductory biology course—we should acknowledge that although we may not always be able to reduce the volume of material that they are expected to learn, we can be sensitive to the impact this may be having on them.

By being aware of what they experience as learners, we can find strategies and interventions to mitigate the effects of the quantity over quality paradigm. For example, we can

- Deemphasize testing to the greatest extent possible and we can develop assessment measures that move away from the model of cram, memorize, regurgitate, and forget
- Make a special point of contextualizing the material we teach so that students can apply it to their everyday lives
- Take into consideration how much work we require students to do in the context of their other classes and obligations so that we place more realistic work demands on them

Whatever strategies we choose, it is important that we remember that holding space for students means also creating the kind of breathing space that can ignite learning. This point is captured perfectly in the poem "Fire" by leadership educator and poet Judy Brown. Brown reminds us that in order for a fire to burn successfully the logs cannot be packed too tightly together, there needs to be adequate space for the flames to flourish.[5]

[handwritten margin note: Fire analogy]

3. DON'T TAKE AWAY STUDENTS' POWER

Students have more power than they realize and certainly more power than we often give them credit for. This sentiment is a central theme of Deborah Meier's classic manifesto for public education, *The Power of Their Ideas*. As the title of her book suggests, students have many great ideas. Regrettably, the structure of schools and the methods of our teaching create situations in which "some children recognized the power of their ideas while others became alienated from their own genius."[6]

Meier asks, "How did schools, in small and unconscious ways, silence these persistent playground intellectuals? Could schools, if organized differently, keep this nascent power alive, extend it, and thus make a difference in what we grow up to be?"[7]

What if as teachers we were to help students recognize the power of their ideas and take steps to ensure that their power is realized? Consider the following example: Ninth-grade mathematics students in Khan Academy's Upside Down Academy Project were offered opportunities to extend their understanding of math concepts by creating teaching videos whereby they would teach about a mathematical concept by explaining how they came to learn and understand that concept. The combination of sharing mathematical knowledge and the use of digital media highlighted their skills and reaffirmed the power of their ideas. Students received peer and teacher feedback, which were then incorporated into second video lessons. By encouraging students to teach as they learn, the Upside Down classroom offers students a space to recognize their own strengths and capacities and subsequently keep their "nascent power alive."[8]

[handwritten margin note: would be awesome]

We can also preserve students' power by honoring their ideas about the educational process. One mechanism for doing this is to offer them opportunities to participate in constructing the rules and guidelines governing classroom activities.

Next, we outline an exercise we use with students to determine the parameters for class discussions in our college classrooms. This exercise can be used with student at all levels. Indeed, even very early elementary classroom teachers hold discussions. It is never too early for students to learn how to share their thoughts and listen to their peers, nor is it ever too early to introduce students to the idea that they too hold some power within the classroom. To that end, we offer suggestions in italics for ways this exercise can be adapted for use with children as young as five or six.

When we use this exercise to determine the parameters for class discussions in our college classrooms, students have emphasized respect, openness, genuine listening, and preparedness as key characteristics for fostering a safe and welcoming classroom space.

၆ა၆ა

EXERCISE: DEVELOPING A DISCUSSION CHARTER[9]

1. Students begin by taking a few notes by themselves on the following questions:
   - Think back to some of your most enjoyable group discussion experiences. Can you identify some of the characteristics of these discussions that made them so enjoyable for you?
   - Think back to some of your least enjoyable group discussion experiences. Can you identify some of the characteristics of these discussions that made them so unpleasant for you?
2. Students then consider their roles while engaged in discussions by completing the following sentences:
   - I know I've contributed usefully to the discussion when I _____.
   - The best way for me to show that I take the discussion seriously is for me to _____.
   - I might remain silent during discussions because _____.
   - I should share my ideas during discussion, even if I feel uncomfortable, because _____.
   - *Adaptation:* For classrooms with children who can't take notes for themselves, on the day before the exercise, teachers can still gather information and prepare students for the in-class exercise described in steps 3 and 4 by individually conferencing with students and taking notes on their responses to the questions in steps 1 and 2. This will show students that you take their contributions seriously, will help the quiet students feel valued and heard, and will avoid the pitfalls of all-class brainstorming. Teachers will want to adapt some of the language in the questions for lower grades.

3. Next, students form groups of three and consider the following prompts:
   - Take turns sharing your responses about what made group discussions enjoyable for you. As a group, identify any overlapping themes and similar experiences, and make a list of characteristics that you all agree should be incorporated into a class.
   - Take turns sharing your responses about what made group discussions unpleasant for you. As a group, identify any overlapping themes and similar experiences, and make a list of characteristics that you all agree should be avoided in class.
   - For the characteristics of enjoyable discussions you identified, consider what things teachers and students could do to ensure that these characteristics are present.
   - For the characteristics of unpleasant discussions you identified, consider what things teachers and students could do to ensure that these characteristics are avoided.
   - *Adaptation:* For very early grades where teachers conferenced individually with students, teachers would share some of the answers students gave to these questions and ask students to get into groups, charging students simply with coming up with ideals and guidelines for making sure discussions are fun and everyone participates.
4. In the final step, go around the room and have members of each group share characteristics they agree lead to productive and safe group discussions. Select a student to write these on the board under the heading "Charter for Discussion." This charter can be posted online if the class has an online course shell associated with it and/or it can be posted in the classroom. Since students created the charter, they have more buy-in than had these expectations been imposed on them without their input. It is helpful to review the charter multiple times throughout the school year, reminding students of their commitments to each other and to co-creating a safe and productive learning environment.

---

4. KEEP YOUR OWN EGO OUT OF IT

As we discuss in Chapter 4, "Leave My Ego at the Door," teachers face a lot of vulnerabilities. Every day we put ourselves on display in front of students, parents, colleagues, and administrators. Many of us would love to be the ones that children run to on the playground and impulsively hug or the ones with the high ratings on Rate My Professor. It is hard not to care about what others think of us.

Professional pride and ego may drive a desire to be viewed as effective, even masterful. But serving students compassionately means that we have to also recognize where our pride and egos are getting in the way. How can we curtail our own sense of self-importance and keep the focus squarely on students' needs?

Because we offer a fuller discussion of leaving our egos behind in chapter 4, here we briefly explore what may on the surface seem like the opposite of holding space for students: having the strength and clarity to say no. Saying no to students, or even "disciplining them with dignity,"[10] may require that we prioritize what's best for the students over what's best for our own self-esteem.

Holding space for students doesn't mean creating wide-open spaces that can expand infinitely. It does not mean letting students do or say whatever they want just so they will appreciate us. It means discerning how much space we can provide, what type of space we are capable of providing, and what types of boundaries we need to set up to hold that space. Brené Brown, who conducts research on vulnerability, compassion, and courage, finds that the most compassionate people are the ones who maintain the clearest boundaries.

Boundaries can be used to express respect and communicate to others the parameters of appropriate and inappropriate behavior. Brown explains that when we let people do things that are hurtful to us, we become resentful and hateful. "I'd rather be loving and generous and very straightforward with what's okay and not okay," Brown says.[11] In the classroom, creating boundaries may look like setting up classroom rules of conduct and reminding students periodically about these rules. It may look like being clear and firm, transparent and fair when administering rules. If we are balancing these boundaries with sincere efforts to give students power and honor their needs as individuals, the result is a safe and predictable space where students can explore with confidence.

5. MAKE STUDENTS FEEL SAFE ENOUGH TO FAIL

Plett writes that failure is "part of the journey and not the end of the world. When we, as their space holders, withhold judgement and shame, [we offer people] the opportunity to reach inside themselves to find the courage to take risks and the resilience to keep going even when they fail."[12]

Every student experiences failures in school; it is inherent to the learning process. And yet for many students, failure is a major source of fear, angst, and pain. To teach with compassion is to let students know that failure is welcome in the classroom. In creating a safe and even inviting space for students to fail we are helping them to unleash their intellectual curiosities and practice beginner's mind without fear of reprisals or reprimands—from teacher and students alike.

One of the easiest and most obvious ways to begin creating a safe environment for failure is to act as a model and not be afraid to show our own shortcomings. If we are struggling with some new technology in front of the class, for example, and unable to get the smart board or PowerPoint presentation working, we have a choice. We can ask openly for help and model using our failure to learn, or we can try to hide and make excuses. When a student poses a challenging question, we can admit that we don't know the answer and model ways to do further research to discover the answer, or we try vainly to supply some kind of response, maybe twisting our answer back to something we do know. Until we feel safe enough to fail in the classroom, and until we stop pretending we know everything or have all the answers, it will be difficult to convince students that failure is welcome here.

We might also want to be open to sharing specific examples of how we failed when we were students such as an exam we didn't pass, a class in which we did poorly, or even an entire subject that we just could not fully grasp. We can even branch out to nonacademic examples and talk about forgetting lines in a school play, getting cut from a sports team, or receiving detention for goofing off with friends.

In sharing our experiences of failing in school, we help to demystify the infallible perception students may have of us (and that we may intentionally or unintentionally promote) that we are infallible and that failure hasn't played a key role in our own success.

Another strategy to consider is to make failure a part of the lesson plan, teaching students that everyone fails and that failure is often essential for success. Pointing to famous people whose failures ended up fueling their success may help illustrate this.

For example, J. K. Rowling was a jobless, penniless, and depressed single mother when she created the storyline for *Harry Potter*. Her own failures and challenges helped her create the courageous characters that have inspired so many young people.

Bill Gates failed at his first business but this failure allowed him to refine his business acumen and helped him become a successful and innovative entrepreneur.

And after unsuccessfully creating a commercially viable lightbulb, Thomas Edison was asked how he handled such failure and he replied that he now knew over two thousand ways an electric lightbulb would not work and that success was imminent.

All of these examples remind us of a point that Brené Brown makes and that we may regularly remind students: "There is no innovation and creativity without failure. Period."[13]

Finally, we can invite students to view the classroom not so much as a place where they are receivers of information and an audience for lessons but more as a laboratory for trying out new things; an incubator to test out ideas, questions, and assumptions; a safe and nonjudgmental place to take risks and learn from their mistakes.

Educator Doug Lemov outlines an approach teachers can use to intentionally shape the classroom as a place where trial and error can happen. He calls this building a culture of error. According to Lemov, creating this culture in the classroom involves doing four things:[14]

1. Expecting error and communicating this expectation to students
2. Withholding the answer to encourage students to engage and grapple with questions
3. Managing your tell, or how you respond, to wrong answers so that you don't unintentionally dismiss a student's effort (how many times have you nodded and said "Ah interesting" in response to an off-target response?) while "pretending" to value risk taking and error
4. Praising risk taking; he suggests using language like, "I love the fact that this is such a hard question and I see so many brave hands in the air" or "Which of these do you think is my favorite wrong answer?"

Lemov makes it clear that teachers must start by first establishing expectations for how students will respond when other students are struggling to come up with an answer, making it clear that the job of class members is not to shine as individuals who can supply the correct answer but to offer patience and support their classmate, thus communicating that the struggle has value in and of itself. Ultimately, our goal in all of these efforts is to remind students that in this classroom they have the opportunity to learn, grow, practice, fail, and try over and over again.

6. GIVE GUIDANCE AND HELP WITH HUMILITY AND THOUGHTFULNESS

Almost all of our interactions with students present opportunities to give guidance, feedback, and encouragement. But nowhere is our feedback more keenly felt than when we evaluate and comment on student work. In this section we focus on strategies for offering evaluative comments with humility and thoughtfulness. We call this *compassionate feedback*.

Learning is often a delicate endeavor and many of us do not think of the fragility of learning as much as we should. Many students lack the confidence to be able to withstand overly harsh criticism and negative reinforcements. Think back to when you were a student and consider if you were able to nonchalantly shrug off comments that questioned your understanding of the material or your ability to write clear sentences.

We have heard from students who have recounted stories of the harsh, demeaning, and insulting feedback they have received from teachers. If we want to teach with compassion we must figure out how to convey criticism to students in a constructive and compassionate manner. Can we push them intellectually without them feeling so demoralized that they reject learning?

The ancient Sufi tradition of the Four Gates of Speech can offer a helpful guide in our efforts to comment with compassion. This tradition advises us to speak only after our words have passed through four gates. The four gates are intended as a sort of litmus test for things we plan to say or write. Before writing comments on students' work or talking to them in a meeting, we may ask ourselves the following questions that are at the entry points to each of the four gates. If we cannot answer yes to any of these four questions then we might consider recomposing our feedback.

Gate 1: Are these words true? Presumably, most of what we write on students' papers is true. For example, we may point out grammatical or mathematical errors, or highlight the incorrect use of a concept or formula. Still, this question is a useful one to ask ourselves to ensure that we do not get too complacent about our own knowledge and self-assuredness.

Gate 2: Are these words necessary? This question, and the following one, really gets at the challenge of offering compassionate feedback. How do we gauge what is necessary and what is not?

One strategy is to use a rubric that details expectations and elements that you will be looking for in your evaluation, preferably one that was shared with students when the work was first assigned. The beauty of the rubric is that it focuses both the teacher and the student on what is important and there are no surprises.

Gate 3: Are these words beneficial? Comments are only beneficial if students can understand them and use them to improve their work. Consider the intention behind your comments, taking care to convey clearly what you mean. Students do not know what is going on in our heads nor do they have our knowledge base. If our only comment is "Rewrite" or "Redo," the student may not know how to make it right or how to redo it.

The point of offering compassionate feedback is to use our comments to promote student learning; we do not want to make comments that leave students befuddled, frustrated, or disheartened. Even if we have many critical evaluations of their work, we should point out these deficiencies in a manner that encourages and does not stunt their further intellectual growth.

Gate 4: Are these words kind? It seems strange to think that some educators would write unkind comments on students' papers but we have heard too many stories from students on the receiving end of such feedback to not mention these. Big block letters that proclaim, "THIS IS WRONG" or "NO!!!" or "ARE YOU KIDDING?" are examples that would fail this fourth gate test.

But these egregious and obvious examples are easy to watch out for. What's more difficult to avoid are the comments made in haste without much thought about how the person on the receiving end might respond, comments that on the surface seem like they should be relatively benign, but that have the power to dishearten and discourage.

When considering this fourth gate, two strategies are helpful. First, always read student work through once before marking it up to get the big picture and to avoid acting on impulse. If time and the sheer number of papers makes this unfeasible, then at least skim the first page or section before settling in to a more thorough read of the whole document.

Second, get in the habit of leading with something positive. It could be an affirmation of the student's effort ("It's clear that you put a lot of work into this paper"), an acknowledgment of their enthusiasm ("I love how you approach this topic with so much excitement and passion"), or a recognition of their critical thinking ("You raise so many relevant points and you make connections to the theories and concepts we're studying"). It also may help to begin comments by addressing students by their names. This demonstrates that your comments begin from a place of thoughtfulness where you see each student as a person and not just a body of work that needs to be processed.

These simple strategies help to humanize the process of offering feedback and can go a long way toward softening the constructive criticism that is about to follow. Admittedly, in offering students feedback it is difficult to follow the old adage that if you don't have anything nice to say, don't say anything. Still, there are things we can do to ensure that we at least provide criticism in a kind and supportive manner.

One last point to consider: Before sharing our feedback with students we can read what we wrote as if we are the student reading these words for the first time. We can ask ourselves, how does it feel to receive this feedback? Is it true, beneficial, necessary, and kind? Would I appreciate and find value in these comments or are they hurtful and discouraging? Considering the message from the student's point of view, much like the whole premise of the Four Gates of Speech, is a way to force ourselves to slow down and be more reflective about the comments we make.

7. CREATE A CONTAINER FOR COMPLEX EMOTIONS, FEAR, TRAUMA, AND SO FORTH

Rumi's famous poem "The Guest House" describes how as humans we are a kind of guest house every day experiencing such new arrivals as "a joy, a depression, a meanness." The poem encourages us to "welcome and entertain them all!" even "the dark thought, the shame, the malice, meet them at the door laughing and invite them in."[15]

Just as our thoughts arrive unexpectedly, so, too, does the arrival of students whose behaviors and attitudes may surprise and bewilder, even anger and annoy us. Rather than grumble about the ones who irritate us, we can treat each one as our guest, welcoming each student into a nourishing learning environment and providing a place of acceptance. Teaching with compassion means acknowledging the humanity within us all and providing the space for learning to occur alongside of and in connection with our human experiences and emotions.[16]

Holding space for challenging emotions in an educational setting doesn't mean we need to act as counselors whose job it is to heal emotional wounds. But it does mean recognizing that our minds are not separate from our emotions and our life experiences; we are human beings, not automatons absorbing information disassociated from emotional responses.

If a student does appear disturbed, we can at the very least acknowledge her or his feelings and offer warmth and understanding. But we should remember that sometimes being warm and compassionate is not enough, and it is necessary to refer a student to others with appropriate training.

Teaching with compassion does not require us to invite students into emotionally vulnerable spaces; however, in response to those students who exhibit this type of vulnerability or who may be open to self-inquiry, there are helpful actions we can take. We can create a safe, nonjudgmental learning environment for students to explore their emotional responses to challenging materials. For example, we can inform students in advance of the nature of the course materials so that they are not surprised by a topic that may uncover deep emotional wounds. And if we are working with materials that some students may find traumatic, we can have support resources readily available so that students don't have to ask for them.

But sometimes we don't need to engage the emotions; just simply acknowledging them is enough. One way of doing this is by beginning class with check-ins, also called "where you're ats."

EXERCISE: WHERE YOU'RE ATS

At the beginning of the class ask students the following: "In a word or phrase, in this moment, where are you at?" There are a number of ways you can structure sharing their response. Students can go around the room and share their inner experience: sleep deprived (a popular one), cranky, enthusiastic, stressed out, joyful, sad, and so forth, or say, "I pass." Or you could take a few suggestions, write them on the board, and have students put check marks next to the ones that apply to them. This gives you a quick visual take on the temperature of the class.

After doing this exercise, lightness often pervades the room and energy seems heightened as we launch into the topic for the class. Having recognized each other as human beings with complex inner lives, a sense of connection among students occurs. Perhaps students recognize that on some level, we are all in this together and they become more open and willing to share their experiences.

---

8. ALLOW STUDENTS TO MAKE DIFFERENT DECISIONS AND TO HAVE DIFFERENT EXPERIENCES THAN YOU WOULD

Students come from all walks of life. Part of holding space for students is to respect the diversity of viewpoints and perspectives that exist in the classroom. We must recognize that students may make alternative choices based on their cultural norms and experiences.

Our way of doing things, even if it is informed by our professional experience and expertise, is still just one possibility of how things might be done. If we can, as Plett writes, "release control"—or, in Karen Armstrong's language of compassion, dethrone ourselves from the center of our universe—then we will be primed to "honor differences" and create possibilities for students to exert their agencies.

There are many ways that we can give students the space to have alternative experiences. Some of these we have already discussed in the previous tips on giving students power and trusting their wisdom.

We would like to use this last section to highlight one of our favorite examples of a teacher truly getting out of the way and letting students determine their own experiences. This teacher, at the end of the school year, invites her elementary students to decide what they would like to do in the final three weeks of class. After a full school year in which the day-to-day routine was dictated by the teacher (and the state-imposed curriculum), the students are given some much needed and much appreciated space to co-create their educational experiences.

Over the years, students have come up with such unique and surprising initiatives as a one-day science fair, a field trip to a kindergarten class to read to them, a dramatic performance for parents, a secret exchange of greeting cards that the students make for each other, a one-day art show with time to draw and hang their work, a class talent show, a research project on animals that is done in pairs, and an extended morning meeting in which another class is invited to take part. Each year the experiences that transpire in this classroom are different because every school year brings forth a fresh and unique group of students.

Teaching with compassion calls us to view ourselves first as facilitators of learning and second as teachers of a particular subject matter. As facilitators of learning, it is our main job to hold space for learning to happen. Whether it is through how we interact with students, how we empower them and draw on their expertise, how we express expectations and create assignments, how we offer feedback, or how we employ pedagogical classroom strategies, holding space provides students opportunities to tap into their experiences, emotions, struggles, and challenges. In short, holding space for students allows them to be fully human in the classroom.

QUESTIONS FOR FURTHER REFLECTION

1. Can you recall an instance where a friend, family member, or teacher held space, offering presence, warmth, and calm as you faced a challenging situation? How did this experience impact you?
2. Think of an instance where you helped someone connect with her own inner wisdom. What did you do, or not do, to foster the development of insight and wisdom in another?

3. How did teachers empower you when you were a student? Has a teacher ever taken your power away? In your life as an educator, what have you done to empower students?

4. Think of the word *boundary*. What other words and images come up when you think of boundaries? Which images have a negative connotation? Which images have a positive connotation? Do you see any patterns regarding how you think about boundaries? In what ways would it be helpful to shift your ways of thinking about and creating boundaries with students?

5. How could you turn your classroom "upside down"? Try it and observe what both you and your students learn from the experience!

·Slides: 5-8
· Conclusion

Chapter Eig

Teach like the

Wanting students to reach their full potential, I radiate warmth across the entire classroom and offer all students my attention.

When Peter first started teaching, he used to walk past a local bookstore on his way to and from campus. One day, there was a window display for a new book of poetry by Mary Oliver with the title poem, "Why I Wake Early," featured on a poster.[1] He stopped to read this short poem and it instantly became one of his favorites.

The poem offers love and appreciation for that great ball of fire in the sky. It begins with a greeting to the sun and recognition of all that this unique star does for us. It offers gratitude to the sun for always brightening our days, comforting us with its warm embrace, and allowing us to start our day on a positive and generous note. It is the type of poem that lightens your mood and brings a smile to your face as soon as you read it.

Like much of Mary Oliver's poetry, this poem encourages us to slow down, take notice, and be more appreciative of the splendors of the natural world. In this case, her attention is on that amazing force of nature that sustains all life on Earth. The sun truly is an incredible phenomenon that many of us probably take for granted.

We can use Mary Oliver's words as a guiding aspiration for our own presence in the classroom. How may we strive to teach like the sun? By effortlessly radiating warmth, indiscriminately dispensing love and generosity, and bringing light and hope to even the most troubled and distressed students. Just as the sun supports all life on earth, so too can teachers support all students who walk through their doors.

Assuming, we would argue wrongly, that teachers only have a finite amount of attention to give, some of us may feel inclined to focus our energies on the troubled students and leave the high achievers on their own; others will ignore the needy or difficult and focus on those we judge to be the most promising. But when we decide to teach like the sun, we do not pick and choose whom we want to help or when we want to help them.

When it comes time to decide on whom, on what, or where to unleash its solar power, the sun does not discriminate. It does not find one group of people or one region of the world more worthy than another; it just shines on whoever and whatever is in its glow. It offers a stable, consistent, and predictable presence much like we might expect of teachers in the classroom.

Whether it is with the insecure student who cannot seem to do anything independently, the unruly student who never follows directions, the ambitious student who is constantly asking for more challenges, or the reticent student who never responds to our overtures, our objective should be to shower our energies and attention fully on the entire class. With nonjudgmental impartiality, we strive to assist all students we encounter with equal kindness, concern, and positive attention.

Echoing this sentiment, Buddhist teacher Judith Lief observes,

True compassion is like the sun, which effortlessly radiates warmth. The sun does not choose who is or is not worthy of receiving sunlight—it shines on everyone. Neither does the sun check for results or seek confirmation. For the sun, shining is not a project, nor is the sun on a mission of mercy. Nonetheless, through its warmth, the entire earth is nourished. The sun is already in the sky. We don't have to worry about putting it there; we simply need to remove the clouds that block us from seeing it.[2]

NOURISHING THE POTENTIAL OF ALL STUDENTS

Part of the reason some students never achieve their full potential is because they fail to receive the encouragement and nourishment they need to thrive. Like a plant that does not receive enough sunlight, the hopes and dreams of these students may eventually wilt and die. When we teach like the sun we consciously and willingly provide students with the sustenance—emotional, social, and intellectual—that will help them grow, make, create, and be. Knowing that students may not be getting this nourishment in other arenas of their lives should make us all the more committed to radiating goodness upon them when they are in our presence.

When we offer students our undivided attention we confirm their existence, telling them they matter, they are important to us, and we care about them. Arguably, this is the most significant lesson we teach students. Despite all of the book knowledge we may impart to them, affirming the value of their existence may be the most important message they learn in school.

Imagine if this message was reinforced throughout all of their years of schooling. As an observation often attributed to the poet e. e. cummings suggests, once one has this conviction, the potential for learning is boundless: "We do not believe in ourselves until someone reveals that something deep inside us is valuable, worth listening to, worthy of our trust, sacred to our touch. Once we believe in ourselves we can risk curiosity, wonder, spontaneous delight or any experience that reveals the human spirit."[3]

In making a case for teaching like the sun, we are not suggesting that teachers are wholly responsible for some students veering far astray from their hopes and dreams. However, we do believe that teachers should do everything in their power to help students stay true to their hopes and dreams. This means honoring students' goals and aspirations, encouraging them to make the life they want for themselves, and providing them with not just the intellectual skills to make their dreams a reality but also the encouragement to stay on their path. All students will experience periods of turbulent and unsettling situations as they make their way from primary to secondary to postsecondary education. As teachers, we can work to ensure that in the time they are with us in the classroom, we do our best to provide them with a nurturing and affirming experience.

SMILE MORE

Like many of the themes we discuss in this book, teaching like the sun might sound like a good idea in principle, but it is not easy to put into practice. The same semester that Peter saw Mary Oliver's poem in the bookstore window, he was teaching in an unappealing classroom that was dark and cold, and he was facing a group of students who, from his clouded perspective, seemed uninterested and unenthusiastic about being there.

In trying to overcome this dreariness and get the class more engaged, he pulled out all of his pedagogical tricks. Nothing seemed to work. At some point, he threw in the towel, let the circumstances get the better of him, and more or less taught on auto-pilot for the rest of the semester. It was an uninspiring class that he was glad to have finished. As he was reading the end-of-semester student evaluations, he came upon one comment that has stayed with him ever since: "SMILE MORE ☺."

Although he always thought of himself as an enthusiastic and energetic educator, when he reflected on this simple bit of constructive criticism he realized the student was absolutely correct. He could have smiled more in that class; he could have smiled a lot more. He let the situation get the better of him and shape his demeanor.

Instead of teaching like the sun, he was teaching like it was a constantly cloudy and rainy day. He was not interested in providing students with emotional warmth or intellectual nourishment; instead, he just wanted to get through those seventy-five minutes and go on with his day. But it was only in that one class that he failed to teach like the sun. In his other two classes, he did smile more, a lot more. He would walk into those classrooms with a sense of excited anticipation, happy to share time and space with the students in those classes.

If we want to teach like the sun, it might help to remember the words of that anonymous student every time we start a new school year or new semester. In fact, "smile more" is a good way to begin and end each and every class.

We are not responsible for the uninviting or uninspiring classroom space, nor can we necessarily determine how the students will react to us. Those things may be largely out of our control. However, the one thing we can control is our own reaction to such circumstances. We can choose how to act, how to respond, and what to feel. We can decide if we want to smile despite all of the problems we have identified. We can remind ourselves that our smile, like the sun, is always there. As Judith Lief says, we just need to remove the clouds that block others from seeing it.

OVERCOMING OUR BIASES

We both know from our own experiences that there may be a tendency to set an arbitrary limit on how helpful you can be to a particular student or to a group of students. Sometimes we may feel as if a student has asked enough questions or taken up enough of our time for one day. We act as if they have used up their allotment of "help" tokens. Through our body language, the shortness of our speech, or the tone of our voice, we essentially tell them to stop bothering us. We shut them down.

It is easy to spot students who are used to this treatment because they often preface their remarks with tentative requests, "Do you mind if I talk to you?" or even with anticipatory apologies, "Sorry to bother you." These students have learned to offer a preemptive mea culpa for being a perceived nuisance.

Some students have even just given up on asking teachers for help. When we focus on teaching like the sun, this approach to dealing with students does not rear its ugly head. There is no compulsion to turn students away, to give them any indication that we are not interested in helping them, or to make them feel as if they are infringing on our precious time.

The points we are making here should not seem too radical because it is actually something that we implicitly expect from many other professions. Think of how you respond when your doctor seems harried and distracted. This is your health after all! So much is at stake; it is unacceptable that she not give you her full and focused attention, that she neglect to follow through on promises, or confuse you with another patient.

Indeed, doctors are trained to practice like the sun—to treat everyone the same, to not pick and choose who is worthy of their care, and to not give top-notch care to some patients and mediocre care to others. This orientation is written into the Hippocratic Oath that all doctors pledge to follow. It is true, of course, that not all doctors fully practice by this ethos but it is encouraging, and maybe even comforting, to know that the Hippocratic Oath exists as a starting point, as a basic set of expectations.

Maybe such an ethos is even more relevant and applicable for educators because young people often find themselves at the mercy of the adult world. School-age children did not choose to be born into poverty or family dysfunction, nor did they choose to suffer from anxiety, depression, ADHD, or any other physical or emotional ailment. Even those who are not deemed "needy" still have social, emotional, and intellectual needs to be met. They still have potential to be realized and aspirations to be fulfilled. So why then isn't teaching with warmth and attention for *all* students a main emphasis of our professional socialization?

One possible reason why teachers-in-training do not spend much time considering how or why to teach like the sun is because it might seem like naive idealism to assume that we could spread compassion over all who walk through our doors. Think about it. Every year we have a new batch of students who enter our lives. Depending on the grade level we teach, the number of students ranges from twenty to more than two hundred. These students come from all walks of life. They are different from us in their tastes, looks, religions, orientations, shapes, and sizes. How could we possibly have compassion for all of these strangers from the moment we encounter them? Is it even realistic to think that we could emit warmth and goodness to this many strangers year after year?

The challenge of cultivating compassion for strangers is not something that we should underestimate. It is a genuinely difficult task no matter how committed one may be to this goal. Thupten Jinpa, a Buddhist monk and scholar who has been the longtime translator for the Dalai Lama, has argued that the capacity to be compassionate may come quite naturally to us when we are talking about our family and loved ones; however, it needs to be more deliberately cultivated when we extend such compassion beyond our immediate circle.[4]

This makes perfect sense. We have a history with our loved ones. We have built bonds, established ties and trust, and expressed and received love from them. Finding a way to be compassionate for the revolving door of strangers over the course of our teaching lives is not so straightforward. And if we want to teach like the sun and emit compassion from day one, then the challenge is even greater. We must, as Jinpa suggests, deliberately cultivate compassion. So what does this mean?

The first step to genuinely cultivating compassion for all students is to acknowledge that we may not treat all of them equally. Let's face it: we all have favorites. Teaching like the sun is not possible unless we can get to the point of identifying such favoritism and preferences. If we are in denial about treating some students with importance while treating others with indifference, then we will only be able to nourish a select group of students and not the entire class.

Sometimes we may not even realize we do this, and other times we may be unwilling to acknowledge it. But the truth is, unless we intentionally make an effort to teach like the sun, it is a very difficult thing to do. For most teachers—including the authors—the typical classroom consists of some students who receive a disproportionate amount of our nourishing rays than others. Our favorite students might get more of our attention, more of our generosity, and more of our smiles.

Students for whom we have an affinity are likely to get more feedback on their work, may be able to push the boundaries of acceptable behavior a little farther, and are more likely to enjoy a personal connection with us. Students with whom we feel less affinity or connection or whom we find irritating are more likely to get less from us. We give them less attention, we may be stricter with them, and we deny them access and insight into who we are.

The Dalai Lama has said, "To feel true compassion for all beings, we must remove any partiality from our attitude toward them. Our normal view of others is dominated by fluctuating and discriminating emotions."[5] This point is an important one to remember as we work toward acknowledging our favoritism. Our feelings for students are not always even and constant. Some days certain students may be on our good side and other days they may be in the proverbial dog house.

When we can accept the impermanence of our feelings toward students then it becomes easier to develop the compassion for all of them. Recognizing the transient nature of our preferences helps us to realize the seeming arbitrariness of who receives our nourishing rays some days but not others. Knowing this to be the case, we can strive to be less discriminating in our day-to-day activities.

If we are serious about wanting to "remove any partiality from our attitude" toward others, then we must confront our own biases, stereotypes, and prejudices. As Cheryl Staats, a senior researcher at the Kirwan Institute for the Study of Race and Ethnicity at Ohio State University, points out, our "unwavering desire to ensure the best for children is precisely why educators should become aware of . . . implicit bias: the attitudes or stereotypes that affect our understanding, actions, and decisions in an unconscious manner."[6]

We need to look inward, be genuinely introspective, and not shy away from seeing things we may not want to admit. Thus, we must own up to the hidden, implicit, and even subconscious assumptions and feelings we have toward others because it is these perceptions that cloud our interactions with them. If we walk into the classroom without being aware of our biases, stereotypes, and prejudices then we will mistakenly, and maybe even indignantly, think that we treat all students fairly, justly, and compassionately.[7]

And let's be frank: what we are talking about here are things like sexism, racism, classism, ableism, homophobia, transphobia, xenophobia, and religious intolerance, to name just a few. We all have some aspect of these deep in the fabric of our being (or maybe not so deep). Even the most well-intentioned, most accepting, and most considerate person is not free from such biases. These -isms of intolerance are ubiquitous. From the moment we are born we are bombarded with images, messages, lessons, examples, and opinions that reflect and reinforce these beliefs. No one is immune to them.

In some respects, the -isms of intolerance may just be the tip of the iceberg when it comes to beliefs that limit and obscure our view of others. As much as we may resist conceding that these societal prejudices are entrenched in our psyche, it may be even more difficult for us to confess to ourselves that there are superficial characteristics that influence how we treat students. A student's personality, height, weight, clothes, attractiveness, accent, speech style, interests, or hobbies may all affect the manner and the extent to which we engage with them.

There are ample social psychological studies and even an entire theoretical framework called *unconscious bias theory* that attest to the influence of these superficial traits when it comes to hiring practices as well as an individual's perceived believability, likability, and honesty.[8] Can we really make the case that teachers are not similarly affected by these subliminal partialities? Can any of us sincerely deny that we have not given some students more favorable attention because of one of these characteristics? Is it truly possible to claim that one walks into the classroom and gives every student the same opportunities for growth, the same undivided attention, the same benefit of the doubt, or the same level of care and concern?

We suspect that the points we are making here may make some readers uncomfortable, defensive, and maybe even angry. We want to elicit these feelings because that likely means that you are deeply invested in how you are teaching (which is also probably why you are reading this book).

Recall the insights of David Whyte discussed in chapter 3, "Learn from Adversity," in which he suggests that "anger is the deepest form of compassion" and the "purest form of care" because it arises out of the perceived threat to the things we want so dearly to protect. Anger reflects our love. When we are asked to admit that we treat some students better than others and then we feel angry at ourselves that we allow this to occur, our reaction is a direct reflection of our deep commitment to "what we belong to, what we wish to protect and what we are willing to hazard ourselves for."[9] If we are genuinely committed to teaching all students with compassion, then it is likely that we feel frustrated and disappointed in ourselves when we realize that we are not successful in achieving this goal.

Research on student learning demonstrates clearly that examining our own assumptions and modeling inclusivity are two key components for successful teaching.[10] But acknowledging our biases, stereotypes, and prejudices is not an easy or natural process. It requires *honesty* so that we can admit these things to ourselves; *compassion* so that we do not berate ourselves over our imperfections; and *forgiveness* so that we allow ourselves to move forward and grow as educators.

ლოგი

EXERCISE: CRITICAL SELF-REFLECTION
THROUGH THE STORY OF YOU

Acknowledging our biases, stereotypes, and prejudices takes work. One exercise that we find helpful is called the Story of You. This exercise only takes about an hour and is a useful tool to begin the process of recognizing our limiting perceptions.

We recommend that you spend no more than five minutes freewriting your response to each of the following twelve questions. You may even want to use a timer to stay on track. The exercise is best done as a solitary endeavor where you know that your answers are not going to be shared with others. This way, you can be honest, genuine, and sincere in your responses, and you do not have to worry about being stigmatized, offending others, or feeling defensive about what you write.

The exercise is purely for you, to inquire within, look yourself in the mirror, and come to know the thoughts and perceptions that may cloud your view. It should go without saying that there are no right or wrong answers, nor is the intention of the exercise to make anyone feel bad, guilty, or embarrassed. As with any exercise in critical self-reflection, the purpose is to help you gain a better understanding of who you are and why you might do the things you do.

1. When you think of the various influences that affected the way you came to see the world, what comes to mind? List as many as you can.
2. What values did your family transmit to you while you were growing up?
3. What were the demographics of the schools you attended and how might those environments have affected your worldview?
4. What were the demographics of the communities you grew up in and how might those environments have affected your worldview?
5. Did your gender provide you with any privileges or obstacles that might have affected your worldview? Explain.
6. Did your race provide you with any privileges or obstacles that might have affected your worldview? Explain.
7. Did your social class grant you any privileges or obstacles that might have affected your worldview? Explain.
8. How might your experiences with physical or mental disability, yours or someone else's, affect your worldview?
9. How did the cultural-historic time period in which you grew up affect your worldview?
10. Identify one specific bias, stereotype, or prejudice that you have. How do you think this belief originated?
11. Can you identify any specific ways that this belief has shaped your actions and behaviors?
12. How might you begin to reject this bias or stereotype and not let it negatively influence your actions and behaviors?

In being truthful with ourselves and observing our own perceptions and patterns of behavior, we find that these partialities lose their power to guide our actions.

❧⊙❧⊙

CHOOSE NOT TO BURN OUT

One of the common concerns we hear when talking to colleagues about compassionate teaching is worry that if they spread such care and concern over all of the students in their presence, and do this year after year, then they will quickly reach the point of mental, emotional, and physical exhaustion. Teaching like the sun by giving all students our nourishing warmth is just not sustainable. They will burn out.

Burnout is one of the main reasons that approximately 17 percent (half a million teachers) of K–12 teachers leave the profession every year in the United States. Vicki Zakrzewski reports that teacher burnout often arises from "the negative emotions and inefficiency they feel around the challenges of managing their students."[11] And as a *Faculty Focus* (a higher education teaching strategy newsletter) special report notes,

> There's plenty about teaching that can make a teacher tired—an unending stream of courses to teach, lots and lots of content to deliver, students who are not always well prepared or motivated to handle the material, courses and assignments to design, student work to grade, course evaluations that can feel like personal attacks, colleagues showing signs of cynicism, budget cuts—it's a long list that seems to grow each semester.[12]

In the face of these stresses, the answer isn't to do less and give less. In their article "Prevent Burnout by Making Compassion a Habit," Annie McKee and Kandi Wiens identify self-compassion as a necessary precursor to offering compassion to others. "If you really want to deal with stress," they advise, "you've got to stop trying to be a hero and start caring for and about yourself."[13] Ultimately, through practicing self-care we become more available to care for others.

So how do we begin the work of developing self-compassion? Kristen Neff identifies three components to practicing self-compassion: self-kindness, recognizing our common humanity, and mindfulness.[14] We will briefly look at each of these components and consider how they may help us develop self-compassion as teachers and keep our suns from burning out.

1. Self-kindness. This means treating ourselves as we would treat a dear friend or loved one. Instead of criticizing yourself for being impatient with a student or raising your voice over a noisy classroom, try talking with yourself as you would a best friend. (Please see chapter 3, "Learn from Adversity," for more on positive self-talk.) For example, you might try saying something like this to yourself: "I know I'm feeling frustrated and annoyed. And that's reasonable given the circumstances that I'm facing right now. I know I'm trying to do my best in the current situation."

The type of self-kindness that we're talking about is not one of pampering ourselves (although this is also needed from time to time, too). The self-kindness we're referring to is about extending warmth, gentleness, and compassion to oneself when experiencing suffering and hardship. So when facing those challenging moments—in teaching or otherwise—try to offer yourself a moment of self-kindness. Try checking in with your emotions and extending some warm inner words of support to yourself. From this place of support and encouragement, you may find yourself in a stronger place from which to both address the situation and offer kindness and compassion to others.

2. Recognize our common humanity. This point encourages us to take a moment to realize that we are not the only teacher having this experience. During troubling times, numerous teachers are also going through something quite similar and feeling quite similar emotions. We are not alone. By tapping into our common experience, we take things less personally and also feel the connection to a greater whole. From this place of connection, self-compassion and compassion for the larger dynamic naturally arise.

Neff recommends creating opportunities for teachers to talk with each other so that they can recognize their common experiences. We add one cautionary note to this: while connecting with others and identifying common experiences can be helpful, it can sometimes lead to the blame game (discussed in chapter 4, "Leave My Ego at the Door").

How may we realize that we're not alone within a positive constructive space that promotes compassion for ourselves and others? One way is to be very clear about your intentions for gathering. Consider gathering not to air grievances but rather to share common experiences with the intention for cultivating self-compassion and compassionate teaching. We further explore the importance of networking and developing communities of support in the concluding chapter.

3. Mindfulness. Founder of Mindfulness-Based Stress Reduction Jon Kabat-Zinn defines mindfulness as "awareness that arises through paying attention, on purpose, in the present moment, non-judgmentally."[15] When we practice mindfulness, we observe thoughts, emotions, and physical sensations arise and pass—without getting attached to them and without judging them.

Mindfulness offers us a space through which to observe what is going on within ourselves. Within the context of practicing self-compassion, Neff defines mindfulness as "taking a balanced approach to our negative emotions so that feelings are neither suppressed or exaggerated."[16] Research indicates that teachers who receive mindfulness training show improvements in stress management, well-being, social-emotional regulation, and relationships with students.[17]

Meena Srinivasan, author of *Teach, Breathe, Learn: Mindfulness In and Out of the Classroom* expresses the power of mindfulness practices for educators this way:

> The more we practice coming back to the present with kind awareness, the easier it actually is to be present—a vital quality for educators. Except for perhaps surgeons, teachers make more decisions during the course of the work day, and the demands of the classroom require us to be able to have simultaneously both expansive and focused attention.[18]

ⱷⱷⱷ

EXERCISE: MINDFULNESS PRACTICE

Here is a basic mindfulness practice that uses the breath as a gateway into present moment, nonjudgmental awareness.

Begin by finding a comfortable position. While it is helpful to remain sitting upright, there is no need to contort your body or otherwise create discomfort as you settle into a position. Find the position that is most comfortable for you.

Gently close your eyes and notice your breathing. Bring your attention to the rise and fall of your abdomen as you breathe in and out, or to the sensations as air moves in and out of your nostrils.

Spend some time focusing on your breathing now. Please be gentle and compassionate with yourself. There is no need to sustain a perfect unwavering focus. Once you sustain some focus, it is time to move to the second phase of the mindfulness practice, the part of the practice that Srinivasan calls "expansive."

Begin to notice any thoughts, feelings, or physical sensations that arise. Watch how such phenomena arise and eventually pass. Notice the thoughts that pass through. Without attaching to a thought and following it on its journey, notice from where it arises and to where it passes. Observe with a sense of curiosity and openness. You may have a tendency to get into the analytic mind—wondering, why am I thinking about that? See if you can simply watch all thoughts, including analytic thoughts, without needing to answer any questions. As you notice your mind getting caught up in thoughts, gently return to your breathing, an anchor into present moment awareness.

Watch any emotions or feelings arise. Perhaps you feel a sense of sadness. Where in the body do you feel that sadness? Is it associated with any thoughts? Just notice, without having to analyze or understand. Continue to connect with your breathing and present-moment awareness.

Notice any physical sensations arise. Perhaps your leg starts itching. Can you notice the desire to scratch the itch without actually scratching it? Also notice the sensations of the itch. Is it a constant unyielding sensation, or does it seem to move around, with an apparent life of its own? Notice other sensations: sounds, smells, feelings of heat and cold. Simply notice without attaching to the stories these sensations activate.

Observe that the arising and passing of experiences are akin to clouds passing through the sky of awareness. Our experiences—thoughts, emotions, and sensations—are like clouds forming temporarily and floating through the expansive sky of awareness. Mindfulness practices ultimately ground us in the present moment of expansive awareness.

When you feel ready, open your eyes and note the quality of your experience.

While we may practice self-compassion in the comfort of our own homes and retrain our minds and hearts to respond to challenging situations or just the day-to-day wear of burnout, Neff also says that teachers can benefit from self-compassion in the midst of a frenzied day, particularly when the storm clouds are threatening to obscure our radiant sunshine: "Self-compassion gives you the calm and clarity you need to get through a tough situation emotionally and do your best—a win-win situation for both teachers and students."[19] Neff concludes, "Self-compassion is often a radically new way of relating to ourselves. Research shows that the more we practice being kind and compassionate with ourselves . . . the more we'll increase the habit of self-compassion."[20]

THE WIND OR THE SUN?

We began this chapter with a reference to a poem from Mary Oliver, and we would like to end with a reference to Aesop's fable of the Wind and Sun. As this story goes, the Wind and the Sun were arguing over who is more powerful. They agreed that whoever could make a traveler take off some clothes would be declared stronger.

First, the Wind tried by blowing the traveler with all its might. But the more the Wind blew, the more tightly the traveler held onto his clothes. Frustrated, the Wind called the Sun to see what it could do. The Sun shined its rays brilliantly upon the traveler enveloping him in warmth until the traveler took off some of his clothes. The moral of this story is that to accomplish our goals it is more powerful to act with kindness and warmth than with harshness and severity.

As teachers, we will not get very far if we act harshly and severely. We cannot force students to learn, to be open to new ideas, to act respectfully, and to care for others. What we *can* do is to treat all of them with warmth, love, and kindness so that they will be more likely to follow our lead. While there is no guarantee that they will listen to us, research has shown that behaving with compassion increases trust, while responding with anger or frustration erodes trust and raises anxiety, thereby impacting creativity and productivity.[21]

We are fortunate to have a never-ending supply of opportunities for practicing how to teach like the sun. We have a new batch of travelers who walk into our classrooms every year. Will we follow the Sun and wrap these students, all students, in supportive warmth and care? Or will we mimic the Wind and try to force these students to bend to our will? The choice is ours.

QUESTIONS FOR FURTHER REFLECTION

1. Teaching like the sun is one metaphor for teaching with compassion. Can you think of other metaphors that might illustrate how to teach with compassion? Do these other metaphors offer additional insights or perspectives?
2. Have you ever had a class or a semester where you felt stymied by the classroom setting and the students in the class? How did these factors negatively affect your teaching? How might the situation have been different if you were teaching like the sun?
3. Can you think of any experiences you have had with other professionals in their jobs when they did not treat you with kindness, not give you their full attention, and not be respectful toward you? How did this make you feel? What was your reaction? Is there anything you can learn from these experiences that applies to your role as an educator?
4. Why do you think we can readily identify the biases, stereotypes, and prejudices of others but find it more difficult to identify these things in ourselves? Knowing this to be true, how might it help us teach and learn with students?
5. Thinking of Aesop's fable of the Wind and the Sun, can you identify a time when you responded to students like the Wind? What were your intentions in acting this way? How might your actions have changed if you took the approach of the Sun?

Conclusion

Teaching with Compassion Is a Social Act

We wrote this book to assist educators as they develop and cultivate compassionate teaching. Admittedly, much of our focus has been on the individual. The Teaching with Compassion Oath explores eight approaches that individual educators can take as they face the stresses and strains and joys of teaching. Yet, the need for more compassionate teaching is not merely based on our personal pursuits, desires, problems, and challenges. It is not simply an individual act of kindness, but a response to larger social issues; as such it is a social act, one that has the power to transform our institutions if we let it.

As sociologists, we have spent much of our professional lives examining the ways in which individuals are influenced by external forces. Instead of pointing our analytical telescope in the direction of the individual and assuming that attitudes, beliefs, and behaviors originate from within, we are trained to look at the social world to see how one's position in a constellation of relationships impacts our actions.

This idea that individual behavior has social origins was articulated most famously in *The Sociological Imagination* by C. Wright Mills.[1] As anyone who has ever taken an introductory sociology class has probably learned, Mills argued that if we really want to understand why people do what they do, then we need to identify and understand how their personal stories connect with larger societal processes. With a sociological imagination we seek to understand the mechanisms though which our biographies are shaped by and ultimately shape the social and historical context in which we live.

If we recognize that we are socially formed creatures, and not individuals who are merely driven by inherent or instinctual needs, then we may also recognize that much of what we experience is shared by others. Often, we may think that our experiences are unique to us. In truth, although they may be uniquely *felt* from our own perspective, it is likely that others have dealt with them too.

This idea reflects a second well-known point that Mills made in his classic text. He drew a distinction between *personal troubles* and *public issues* to demonstrate that many of the challenges we face are really social hurdles and not individual obstacles. Mills identified such things as divorce and unemployment and argued that if just one person experienced these things then it would be a personal trouble. But if we live in a society where nearly half of all marriages end in divorce and millions of people are unemployed, then we are really talking about a public issue.

Divorce and unemployment are certainly experienced personally by individuals who face them. However, if as a society we want work to reduce the number of divorces or the number of people who are unemployed, then we need to look to social solutions, not individual or personal ones.

We also recognize that if we want to make the educational process a more humanizing and humanistic endeavor, as we detail throughout this book, then we need to think about compassion as more than just an individual act of kindness. Teaching with compassion is a social act because it counteracts the dehumanizing tendencies of a large-scale bureaucratized institution.

To borrow from another influential sociologist, Max Weber recognized long ago that bureaucracies tend to move in ever more efficient, predictable, calculable, and ultimately dehumanizing directions. As educational institutions strive to become more efficient, cost effective, productive, and calculable (through, for example, an emphasis on quantity over quality, an overreliance on assessments and accountability, and a belief that success can be measured by test scores), there is a tendency to lose touch with the human dimension of teaching and learning.

Teaching with compassion and developing other prosocial behaviors such as perspective taking and empathy cannot be overemphasized if our goal is to help students grow, develop, thrive, and be able to positively contribute to the world around them.

In this sense, we teach with compassion not only for ourselves, but as an act of service for others. Our individual actions have broad social impacts—something that social scientists are beginning to uncover. For example, in *Connected: The Surprising Power of Our Social Networks and How They Shape Our Lives*, Nicholas Christakis and James Fowler offer evidence of the ways in which our influence extends beyond those with whom we come into direct contact and affects those with whom we have never even met: "We discovered that if your friend's friend's friend gained weight, you gained weight. We discovered that if your friend's friend's friend stopped smoking, you stopped smoking. And we discovered that if your friend's friend's friend became happy, you became happy."[2]

Christakis and Fowler have found that for any behavior—whether prosocial like compassion, empathy, and altruism, or antisocial like discrimination, hatred, and violence—our behaviors reach out three degrees (to our friends' friends' friends). Are there invisible connectors that connect us with each other? Do we live within a field of interconnection? We don't know how this works, but nevertheless, the evidence is stunning. We no doubt live within a web of connections.

CULTIVATING COMPASSION IN OUR SCHOOLS

Admittedly, some of us may be more inclined and better equipped to teach with compassion because we have had life experiences that have encouraged and cultivated this orientation. For those who feel less equipped, we hope that the exercises sprinkled throughout this book offer helpful tools and strategies through which to develop these skills.

The key point to remember here is that with the right intention and motivation, along with some institutional supports, resources, and guidance, *everyone* can teach with compassion. Instead of seeing our methods of teaching and learning as uniquely individual choices, we can recognize that they are reflections of the educational landscapes in which we exist. Much like the way that our individual disposition may change when we wake up to a beautiful sunny day after a week of cold, rainy weather, so too will our approach to teaching and learning change if we create the conditions that encourage alternative pedagogies.

To that end, we offer educators these final suggestions as you help create environments and structures that foster and further support teaching with compassion.

THREE WAYS TO CULTIVATE TEACHING
WITH COMPASSION IN YOUR SCHOOL

Our recommendations are based on the spirit of the Buddhist sangha. *Sangha* is a Pali and Sanskrit word that means assembly, company, or community. Thich Nhat Hanh describes the sangha as a community of friends who practice together to bring about and maintain awareness, understanding, acceptance, harmony, and love. He further explains,

> The sangha is not a place to hide in order to avoid your responsibilities. The
> sangha is a place to practice for the transformation and the healing of self and

society. When you are strong, you can be there in order to help society. If your society is in trouble, if your family is broken, if your church is no longer capable of providing you with spiritual life, then you work to take refuge in the sangha so that you can restore your strength, your understanding, your compassion, your confidence. And then in turn you can use that strength, understanding and compassion to rebuild your family and society, to renew your church, to restore communication and harmony. This can only be done as a community—not as an individual, but as a sangha.[3]

1. Develop a Community of Support

As with the sangha, we encourage readers to develop a community of support and practice among colleagues, administrators, family, friends, and so forth. Teaching with compassion is not always easy. At times, it may take an emotional toll on us. A community of support provides encouragement, helping us refuel when we feel drained, and reminds us of why we do what we do—especially when the work is challenging or goes against the cultural norm.

Networks of collegial support facilitate the sharing of resources, collaborating on workshops and projects that help support and engage compassionate teaching. Communities of support may also help us process our experiences together, alleviating a sense of isolation that often arises when we attempt to do something different. At the same time, groups of like-minded individuals can help provide some much-needed relief from the daily challenges—through supporting each other, sharing ideas and experiences, or connecting in other ways, even outside of teaching (like finding a common hobby) to relieve some of the pressure.

Some other ways you may begin developing a community of support include the following:

- Create opportunities for dialogue. Develop and maintain dialogue with one another about compassionate teaching. Whether it is in person, online, or even through journals, continued conversation about experiences and challenges around teaching with compassion provides opportunities for a rich exchange of ideas and practices from which compassionate teaching can grow and thrive.
- Create informal brown-bag luncheons with a focus on teaching with compassion. Ask questions such as, what does compassion mean to you? What does teaching with compassion look like? What are your experiences with teaching with compassion? What are some challenges you face?
- Create Facebook, LinkedIn, or other social networking groups for your school or institution with a focus on compassion.

2. Build Compassionate Schools

In *The Heart of Learning and Teaching: Compassion, Resiliency, and Academic Success*, Ray Wolpow and colleagues define a *compassionate school* as "a school where staff and students learn to be aware of the challenges faced by others. They respond to the physical, emotional, and social challenges faced by students and families by offering support to remove barriers to learning. They do not judge the situations or responses to others. They seek to understand and support."[4]

Building such schools requires leadership, vision, and teamwork. Begin small but start somewhere. You might consider hosting a listening forum with the purpose of helping divergent groups understand each other's experiences and open up the lines of communication. A listening forum is a mediated conversation that provides for opportunities for everyone involved to share their perspectives and be listened to. The idea is not to solve a problem, but to bring all parties to the table and offer all involved a chance to both share their perspectives and hear alternative perspectives.

Even asking your school to sponsor a workshop on teaching with compassion can snowball into larger opportunities. As we build compassion into our institutional structures, such as developing teaching with compassion workshops, learning communities, and conferences, we infuse compassion as a core principle into our schools.

3. Help Build a Culture of Compassion

Building a culture of compassion is about developing educational communities that prioritize the care and well-being of all members. A culture of compassion emphasizes appreciation and support of each other, accentuates creative and collaborative problem solving, and recognizes our inherent interdependence.

To build a community of compassion, consider the following:

- Explore. Ask yourself and others questions such as, what would it take to make care and compassion a priority within our classrooms and schools? What resources would we need to facilitate the individual, institutional, and cultural changes to make compassion a defining feature of teaching and learning?
- Model. Role model compassion both inside and outside of the classroom. But remember, compassion is not an identity we wear as a badge of honor; compassion is a response to suffering. Model compassionate behavior through the way you talk, respond to another's pain, offer feedback, face challenging situations, structure your classroom, and so forth.

- Continue. Bring speakers, workshop facilitators, and others who can offer models of compassion to your schools. Attend compassion conferences and workshops and share information with your colleagues.
- Speak compassion. Seek opportunities to infuse the language of compassion into your school or institution's mission, goals, visions, objectives, and assessment tools. Learn to speak the language of compassion. Marshall Rosenberg, founder of the Center for Nonviolent Communication (NVC), identifies nonviolent communication as a language of compassion. He writes,

> NVC guides us in reframing how we express ourselves and hear others. Instead of habitual, automatic reactions, our words become conscious responses based firmly on awareness of what we are perceiving, feeling, and wanting. We are led to express ourselves with honesty and clarity, while simultaneously paying others a respectful and empathic attention. In any exchange, we come to hear our own deeper needs and those of others.[5]

Cultivating communities of support, infusing compassion into institutional structures, and helping to develop a culture of compassion are all ways that we may carve out niches within our educational institutions for the exploration, development, and support of compassionate teaching.

We want to end by returning to the first line of this book, a quote by the Dalai Lama: "Compassion is the radicalism of our time." In a world where students must navigate increased bureaucratization and decreased humanization, where they are often seen as test scores and not human beings, where increased technologies result in decreased personal contact, and where abuses of power, violence, and a culture of fear are on the rise, the need for compassionate teachers who can help students tap into their gifts, strengths, and passions and promote their well-being is all the more imperative.

Teaching with compassion is a radical and courageous act. It challenges the dehumanizing tendencies of institutional frameworks, it places care and concern for others as central to the craft of teaching, and it challenges the norms of intellectualization and standardization removed from the real lives of students.

Your commitment to teaching and to the growth and well-being of students is valuable beyond anything any one student or individual can reflect back to you. We each do our best amid deep challenges, and ultimately we make a critical difference in the lives of many.

With a deep bow of gratitude, we thank all those reading this book for the many small and large ways you bring compassion into this world, into education, and into the lives of so many.

Notes

PREFACE

1. UNESCO. 1996. *What Makes a Good Teacher?* Retrieved May 9, 2016 (http://unesdoc.unesco.org/images/0010/001041/104124M.pdf).

2. Cochran-Smith, Marilyn, and Kenneth M. Zeichner, eds. 2005. *Studying Teacher Education: The Report of the AERA Panel on Research and Teacher Education*. Washington, D.C.: American Educational Research Association.

3. Jones, Stephanie M., and Jennifer Kahn. 2017. *The Evidence Base for How We Learn: Supporting Students' Social, Emotional, and Academic Development*. The Aspen Institute. Retrieved January 4, 2018 (https://assets.aspeninstitute.org/content/uploads/2017/09/SEAD-Research-Brief-9.12_updated-web.pdf).

4. Seppala, Emma. 2015. "Why Compassion Is a Better Managerial Tactic than Toughness." *Harvard Business Review*, May 7. Retrieved May 17, 2016 (https://hbr.org/2015/05/why-compassion-is-a-better-managerial-tactic-than-toughness).

5. Palmer, Parker. 1998. *The Courage to Teach: Exploring the Inner Landscape of a Teacher's Life*. San Francisco, CA: Jossey-Bass, p. 11.

6. Keltner, Dacher, Jason Marsh, and Jeremy Adam Smith, eds. 2010. *The Compassion Instinct: The Science of Human Goodness*. New York: Norton.

INTRODUCTION

1. Eiseley, Loren. 1979. *The Star Thrower*. New York: Harvest Books.

2. Lief, Judith. 2014. "The Path of Compassion." In *Radical Compassion: Shambhala Publications Authors on the Path of Boundless Love*. Boston, MA: Shambhala.

3. Gould, Stephen Jay. 1992. *Ever Since Darwin: Reflections in Natural History*. New York: Norton, p. 257.

4. Kukk, Christopher L. 2017. *The Compassionate Achiever: How Helping Others Fuels Success*. New York: HarperOne, p. 14.

5. Armstrong, Karen. 2010. *Twelve Steps to a Compassionate Life*. New York: Knopf, pp. 6–7.

6. For more on this see Snyder, C. R., Shane J. Lopez, and Jennifer T. Pedrotti. 2011. *Positive Psychology: The Scientific and Practical Exploration of Human Strengths*. Thousand Oaks, CA: SAGE.

7. Hochschild, Arlie Russel. 1983. *The Managed Heart: Commercialization of Human Feeling*. Berkeley: University of California Press.

8. From Solomon, Erric. 2013. "Tania Singer, PhD: Overcoming Compassion Fatigue." Retrieved January 7, 2018 (http://whatmeditationreallyis.com/index.php/lang-en/home-blog/item/1595-tania-singer-phd-the-myth-of-compassion-fatigue.html). See also Klimecki, Olga M., Susanne Leiberg, Matthieu Ricard, and Tania Singer. 2014. "Differential Pattern of Functional Brain Plasticity after Compassion and Empathy Training." *Social Cognitive Affective Neuroscience* 9(6): 873–879.

9. Ponlop, Dogchen. 2010. *Rebel Buddha: On the Road to Freedom*. Boston, MA: Shambhala, p. 111.

10. Dalai Lama. 2009. *The Art of Happiness in a Troubled World*. New York: Random House, p. 331.

11. Ponlop, *Rebel Buddha*, p. 106.

12. Thomas, P. L., Paul R. Carr, Julie A. Gorlewski, Brad J. Porfilio, eds. 2015. *Pedagogies of Kindness and Respect: On the Lives and Education of Children*. New York: Peter Lang.

13. Thompson, Becky. 2017. *Teaching with Tenderness: Toward an Embodied Practice*. Urbana: University of Illinois Press.

14. Noddings, Nel. 2005. *The Challenge to Care in Schools: An Alternative Approach to Education*, 2nd ed. New York: Teachers College Press.

15. The following books are representative of this publishing trend: *Mindful Teaching and Teaching Mindfulness* by Deborah Schoeberlein (Wisdom, 2009); *The Mindful Teacher* by Elizabeth MacDonald and Dennis Shirley (Teacher's College Press, 2009); *Tuning In: Mindfulness in Teaching and Learning* by Irene McHenry and Richard Brady, editors (Friends Council on Education 2009); *Teach, Breathe, Learn: Mindfulness In and Out of the Classroom* by Meena Srinivasan (Parallax Press, 2010); *The Way of Mindful Education: Cultivating Well-Being in Teachers and Students* by Daniel Rechtschaffen (W. W. Norton, 2014); *Mindful Teaching and Learning: Developing a Pedagogy of Well-Being* by Karen Ragoonaden and Tom Bassarear (Lexington Books, 2015); *Mindfulness for Teachers: Simple Skills for Peace and Productivity in the Classroom* by Patricia Jennings (W. W. Norton, 2015); *Mindful Learning: Reduce Stress and Improve Brain Performance for Effective Learning* by Craig Hassed and Richard Chambers (Shambhala, 2014); *Integrating Mindfulness into Anti-Oppression Pedagogy* by Beth Berila (Routledge, 2016); and *Mindfulness: How School Leaders Can Reduce Stress and Thrive on the Job* by Caryn Wells (Rowman & Littlefield, 2016).

CHAPTER 1

1. Suzuki, Shunryu. 1993. *Zen Mind, Beginner's Mind.* New York: Weatherhill, p. 21.

2. Erikson, Erik. 1958. *Young Man Luther: A Study in Psychoanalysis and History.* New York: Norton, p. 70.

3. Freire, Paulo. 1998. *Pedagogy of Freedom: Ethics, Democracy and Civic Courage.* Lanham, MD: Rowman and Littlefield, p. 89.

4. Freire, *Pedagogy of Freedom,* pp. 37–38.

5. Freire, *Pedagogy of Freedom,* p. 65.

6. Ashley, Dana M. 2016. "It's about Relationships: Creating Positive School Climates." *American Educator* (Winter 2015–2016): 13–16.

7. O'Reilley, Mary Rose. 1984. "The Peaceable Classroom." *College English* 46(2): 103–112.

8. Many commentators have spoken about how busy we are. See, for example, Kreider, Tim. 2012. "The Busy Trap." *Opinionator* (*New York Times* blog), June 30. Retrieved January 11, 2018 (https://opinionator.blogs.nytimes.com/2012/06/30/the-busy-trap/). Holch, Gabor. 2014. "Why Is Everyone So Busy?" *Economist*, December 20. Retrieved January 11, 2018 (https://www.economist.com/news/christmas-specials/21636612-time-poverty-problem-partly-perception-and-partly-distribution-why).

9. See, for example, Grolnick, Wendy S. 2008. *Pressured Parents, Stressed-Out Kids: Dealing with Competition While Raising a Successful Child.* New York: Prometheus. Pope, Denise, Maureen Brown, and Sarah Miles. 2013. *Overloaded and Underprepared: Strategies for Stronger Schools and Healthy, Successful Kids.* San Francisco, CA: Jossey-Bass. Rosenfeld, Alvin, and Nicole Wise. 2001. *The Over-Scheduled Child: Avoiding the Hyper-Parenting.* New York: St. Martins. Thompson, Michael. 2005. *The Pressured Child: Freeing Our Kids from Performance Overdrive and Helping Them Find Success in School and Life.* New York: Ballantine.

10. Twenge, Jean M. 2015. "Time Period and Birth Cohort Differences in Depressive Symptoms in the U.S., 1982–2013." *Social Indicators Research* 121: 437–454.

CHAPTER 2

1. Armstrong, Karen. 2010. *Twelve Steps to a Compassionate Life.* New York: Knopf, p. 9.

2. Phillips, Adam, and Barbara Taylor. 2010. *On Kindness.* New York: Picador, pp. 9–10.

3. Freire, Paulo. 1970. *Pedagogy of the Oppressed.* New York: Continuum, p. 28.

4. Dance, L. Janelle. 2008. "Helping Students See Each Other's Humanity." Pp. 56–60 in *Everyday Antiracism: Getting Real about Race in Schools*, edited by Mica Pollock. New York: New Press.

5. Malala Yousafzai speech to the United Nations. Retrieved June 6, 2017 (http://www.un.org/News/dh/infocus/malala_speach.pdf).

6. "Universal Declaration of Human Rights." United Nations. Retrieved June 6, 2017 (http://www.un.org/en/universal-declaration-human-rights/).

7. Mann, Jonathan. 1998. "Dignity and Health: The UDHR's Revolutionary First Article." *Health and Human Rights* 3: 30–38.

8. Solnit, Rebecca. 2014. *Men Explain Things to Me*. Chicago, IL: Haymarket. Solnit acknowledges that it was an anonymous blogger who coined the term *mansplaining* after reading Solnit's essay.

9. Freire, *Pedagogy of the Oppressed*.

10. Freire, Paulo. 1998. *Pedagogy of Freedom: Ethics, Democracy, and Civic Courage*. Lanham, MD: Rowman & Littlefield, p. 49.

11. Mann, "Dignity and Health," 34.

12. Mann, "Dignity and Health," 37.

13. Hanh, Thich Nhat. 2014. *No Mud, No Lotus: The Art of Transforming Suffering*. Berkeley, CA: Parallax Press, p. 92.

CHAPTER 3

1. Boyle, Gregory. 2011. *Tattoos on the Heart: The Power of Boundless Compassion*. New York: Free Press, p. 179.

2. Cliatt-Wayman, Linda. 2015. "How to Fix a Broken School? Lead Fearlessly, Love Hard." TED video. Retrieved August 18, 2017 (https://www.ted.com/talks/linda_cliatt_wayman_how_to_fix_a_broken_school_lead_fearlessly_love_hard).

3. Cliatt-Wayman, "How to Fix a Broken School?"

4. Gilbert, Paul. 2009. *The Compassionate Mind: A New Approach to Life's Challenges*. Oakland, CA: New Harbinger Publications, p. 75.

5. Kristen Neff. 2013. "The Space between Self Esteem and Self Compassion: Kristin Neff at TEDxCentennialParkWomen." TEDx Talk posted on YouTube, February 6. Retrieved April 6, 2017 (https://www.youtube.com/watch?v=IvtZBUSplr4).

6. Parke, Simon. 2009. *Conversations with . . . Meister Eckhart*. Guilford, UK: White Crow Books, Kindle Edition.

7. For further elaboration on RAIN, please see Brach, Tara. 2004. *Radical Acceptance: Embracing Your Life with the Heart of a Buddha*. New York: Bantam.

8. Hanh, Thich Nhat. 2002. *Anger: Wisdom for Cooling the Flames*. New York: Riverhead Books, p. 30.

9. Hanh, *Anger*, p. 32.

10. Whyte, David. 2015. *Consolations: The Solace, Nourishment and Underlying Meaning of Everyday Words*. Langley, WA: Many Rivers Press.

11. Joyce, James. 1914/1999. *Dubliners*. Hertfordshire, UK: Wordsworth Editions Ltd., p. 77.

12. Brach, Tara. 2013, spring. "Finding True Refuge." *Tricycle*. Retrieved May 23, 2018 (https://tricycle.org/magazine/finding-true-refuge), para. 16.

13. Hanson, Rick. 2009. *Buddha's Brain: The Practical Neuroscience of Happiness, Love, and Wisdom*. Oakland, CA: New Harbinger Publications, p. 121.

14. Hanson, *Buddha's Brain*, p. 173.

15. Palmer, Parker. 1998. *The Courage to Teach: Exploring the Inner Landscape of a Teacher's Life.* San Francisco, CA: Jossey-Bass, p. 42.

16. See Christakis, Nicholas A., and James H. Fowler. 2011. *Connected: The Surprising Power of Our Social Networks and How They Shape Our Lives—How Your Friends' Friends' Friends Affect Everything You Feel, Think, and Do.* New York: Back Bay Books.

17. Hanson, *Buddha's Brain*, p. 138.

18. Hanson, *Buddha's Brain*, p. 138.

19. Hanson, *Buddha's Brain*, p. 169.

20. Morales, Aurora L. 1999. *Medicine Stories: History, Culture, and the Politics of Integrity.* Brooklyn, NY: South End Press, p. 112.

21. Kabat-Zinn, Jon. 2006. *Coming to Our Senses: Healing Ourselves and the World through Mindfulness.* New York: Hachette Books.

CHAPTER 4

1. Sweeny, Camille, and Josh Gosfield. 2013. "What a High School Teacher Who Turned Her Students into Best-Selling Authors Teaches Us about Innovation." *Fast Company*, September 23. Retrieved January 6, 2018 (https://www.fastcompany.com/3017967/what-a-high-school-teacher-who-turned-her-students-into-bestselling-authors-teaches-u).

2. Excerpts from this section were published previously in Kaufman, Peter. 2010. "The Zero Sum Game of Denigrating Students." *Encounter: Education for Meaning and Social Justice* 23(1): 38–45. We appreciate the permission of the publisher to reproduce some of this work.

3. hooks, bell. *Teaching to Transgress: Education as the Practice of Freedom.* New York: Routledge, p. 21.

4. Brach, Tara. 2004. *Radical Acceptance: Embracing Your Life with the Heart of a Buddha.* New York: Bantam, p. 4.

5. Brach, *Radical Acceptance*, p. 4.

6. Whyte, David. 2014. *Consolations: The Solace, Nourishment and Underlying Meaning of Everyday Words.* Langley, WA: Many Rivers Press, p. 233.

7. Chickering, Arthur W., and Zelda F. Gamson. 1987. "Seven Principles for Good Teaching in Undergraduate Education." *The American Association for Higher Education Bulletin*, March, pp. 3–7.

8. Brach, *Radical Acceptance*, p. 4.

9. Lama Surya Das. 2015. *Make Me One with Everything: Buddhist Meditations to Awaken from the Illusion of Separation.* Boulder, CO: Sounds True, p. 54.

10. A teacher shared this with the authors for use in the book with the condition that she remain anonymous.

CHAPTER 5

1. Turkle, Sherry. 2012. *Alone Together: Why We Expect More from Technology and Less from Each Other*. New York: Basic Books.

2. Kaufman, Peter. 2013. "Scribo Ergo Cogito: Reflexivity through Writing." *Teaching Sociology* 41(1): 70–81.

3. Ford, Donna. 2010. "Culturally Responsive Classrooms: Affirming Culturally Different Gifted Students." *Gifted Child Today* 33(1): 50.

4. Deyhle, Donna. 2008. "What Is on Your Classroom Wall? Problematic Posters." Pp. 191–194 in *Everyday Antiracism: Getting Real about Race in Schools*, edited by Mica Pollock. New York: New Press.

5. See, for example, Finley, Todd and Blake Wiggs. 2016. *Rethinking Classroom Design: Create Student-Centered Learning Spaces for 6–12th Graders*. Lanham, MD: Rowman & Littlefield.

6. Janine learned about the Learning Café many years ago. The exercise and the accompanying handout are connected to the idea of a World Café—a methodology for facilitating dialogue among a large number of participants. For more information see http://www.theworldcafe.com/key-concepts-resources/world-cafe-method/.

7. de Tocqueville, Alexis. 2000. *Democracy in America*. New York: Bantam, p. 704.

8. Noguera, Pedro A. 2008. "What Discipline Is For: Connecting Students to the Benefits of Learning." Pp. 132–137 in *Everyday Antiracism: Getting Real about Race in Schools*, edited by Mica Pollock. New York: New Press, p. 132.

9. Carter, Dorinda J. 2008. "On Spotlighting and Ignoring Racial Group Members in the Classroom." Pp. 230–234 in *Everyday Antiracism: Getting Real about Race in Schools*, edited by Mica Pollock. New York: New Press, p. 233.

10. Two useful resources to be an antiracism educator in an antiracist classroom are Pollock, Mica, ed. 2008. *Everyday Antiracism: Getting Real about Race in Schools.* New York: New Press. Moore, Eddie Jr., Ali Michael, and Marguerite W. Penick-Parks. 2018. *The Guide for White Women Who Teach Black Boys*. Thousand Oaks, CA: Corwin.

11. Stephen Brookfield's work in this area is particularly informative. See, for example, Brookfield, Stephen. 1995. *Becoming a Critically Reflective Teacher*. San Francisco, CA: Jossey-Bass. Brookfield, Stephen. 2006. *The Skillful Teacher: On Technique, Trust, and Responsiveness in the Classroom*. San Francisco, CA: Jossey-Bass.

12. Perry, Pamela. 2008. "Creating Safe Spaces in Predominantly White Classrooms." Pp. 226–229 in *Everyday Antiracism: Getting Real about Race in Schools*, edited by Mica Pollock. New York: New Press, p. 227.

13. Perry, "Creating Safe Spaces in Predominantly White Classrooms," p. 227.

14. hooks, bell. 1994. *Teaching to Transgress: Education as the Practice of Freedom*. New York: Routledge, p. 40.

15. Armstrong, Karen. 2010. *Twelve Steps to a Compassionate Life*. New York: Knopf, p. 8.

16. Nussbaum, Martha. 1996. "Compassion: The Basic Social Emotion." *Social Philosophy and Policy* 31(1): 28.

17. For a fuller description of this exercise, see Kaufman, Peter. 2011. "The Similarities Project." *Everyday Sociology Blog*, December 5. Retrieved January 9, 2018 (http://www.everydaysociologyblog.com/2011/12/the-similarities-project.html)

CHAPTER 6

1. See Nathan, Rebekah. 2006. *My Freshman Year: What a Professor Learned by Becoming a Student*. New York: Penguin Books.

2. Zakrzewski, Vicki. 2012. "Four Ways Teachers Can Show They Care." *Greater Good Magazine*, September 8. Retrieved January 19, 2017 (http://greatergood .berkeley.edu/article/item/caring_teacher_student_relationship).

3. Zakrzewski, "Four Ways Teachers Can Show They Care," para. 4.

4. Northern Illinois University's interest inventory—based on school interests, extracurricular activities, and general interest—provides a useful example for those who want to create their own interest inventories. Northern Illinois University. N.d. Student Interest Inventory. Retrieved January 11, 2007 (http://www.niu.edu/eteams/ pdf_s/VALUE_StudentInterestInventory.pdf).

5. Zakrzewski, "Four Ways Teachers Can Show They Care."

6. Derber, Charles. 2000. *The Pursuit of Attention: Power and Ego in Everyday Life*. New York: Oxford.

7. Zerubavel, Eviatar. 2007. *The Elephant in the Room: Silence and Denial in Everyday Life*. New York: Oxford.

8. More, Arthur J. 1989. "Native Indian Learning Styles: A Review for Researchers and Teachers." *Journal of American Indian Education*, special edition, pp. 15–28.

9. Cain, Susan. 2012. *Quiet: The Power of Introverts in a World that Can't Stop Talking.* New York: Crown Publishers, p. 252.

10. Cain, *Quiet*, p. 253.

11. Kohl, Herbert R. 1991/2016. *I Won't Learn from You: The Role of Assent in Learning*. New York: New Press.

12. Kohl, *I Won't Learn from You*, p. 11.

13. This exercise was shared with the authors as part of private correspondence.

14. Derber, *Pursuit of Attention*, p. 97.

15. Caldwell, Martha. 2017. "How to Listen with Compassion in the Classroom." *Greater Good Magazine*, January 30. Retrieved February 17, 2017 (http://greatergood .berkeley.edu/article/item/how_to_listen_with_compassion_in_the_classroom).

16. Caldwell, "How to Listen with Compassion in the Classroom."

17. Briskin, Alan and Sheryl Erickson. 2009. *The Power of Collective Wisdom and the Trap of Collective Folly*. San Francisco, CA: Berrett-Koehler Publishers, pp. 42–43.

18. Hanh, Thich Nhat. 2016. *Silence: The Power of Quiet in a World Full of Noise*. San Francisco, CA: HarperOne, p. 185.

CHAPTER 7

1. Plett, Heather. 2015. "What Does It Mean to 'Hold Space' for People, Plus 8 Tips on How to Do It Well." HeatherPlett.com, March 11. Retrieved November 20, 2015 (http://heatherplett.com/2015/03/hold-space/).

2. Buttice, Chase. 2014. "The Wild Inside: Creative Possibilities for Positive Social Change." Thesis Manuscript. Northern Arizona University, Department of Sociology and Social Work, p. 85.

3. Spielberger, Charles D., William D. Anton, and Jeffrey Bedell. 2016. "Chapter 10: The Nature and Treatment of Text Anxiety." Pp. 317–346 in *Emotions and Anxiety: New Concepts, Methods and Applications*, edited by Marvin Zuckerman and Charles D. Spielberger. East Sussex, England: Psychology Press.

4. See Robert Bjork's Learning and Forgetting Lab at UCLA: https://bjorklab .psych.ucla.edu/research/.

5. Brown, Judy. 2016. *"The Sea Accepts All Rivers" and Other Poems*. Bloomington, IN: Trafford, p. 34.

6. Meier, Deborah. 1995. *The Power of Their Ideas: Lessons for America from a Small School in Harlem.* Boston, MA: Beacon, p. 3.

7. Meier, *The Power of Their Ideas*, p. 3.

8. Chase, Kiera. 2012. "When Students Do the Teaching." *Edutopia* (blog), October 16. Retrieved September 9, 2016 (http://www.edutopia.org/blog/blended -learning-students-teach-students-envision-schools).

9. Exercise adapted from Brookfield, Stephen D., and Stephen Preskill. 2005. *Discussion as a Way of Teaching: Tools and Techniques for Democratic Classrooms*. San Francisco, CA: Jossey-Bass, pp. 54–55.

10. Curwin, Richard L., Allen N. Mendler, and Brian D. Mendler. 2008. *Discipline with Dignity: New Challenges, New Solutions.* Alexandria, VA: Association for Supervision and Curriculum Development.

11. Brown, Brené. 2016. "Brené Brown: Boundaries, Empathy, and Compassion." YouTube video. Retrieved June 10, 2016 (https://www.youtube.com/watch ?v=vSbOlas6jFc).

12. Plett, "What Does It Mean to 'Hold Space.'"

13. Ibid.

14. Doug Lemov. N.d. *Culture of Error*. Retrieved January 6, 2018 (https://www .wiley.com/legacy/downloads/CultureofError_Ebook.pdf). Get the free eBook and see an example of a culture of error in action.

15. Rumi. 2004. *The Essential Rumi*. New York: Harper, p. 109.

16. Importantly, teaching with compassion does not mean condoning violence or injustice as discussed in chapter 3, "Learn from Adversity." In the case of threatening or inappropriate behaviors, it is important to direct students to appropriate support systems and set up clear guidelines for acceptable classroom behavior.

CHAPTER 8

1. Oliver, Mary. 2004. *Why I Wake Early*. Boston, MA: Beacon.

2. Lief, Judith. 2014. "The Path of Compassion." In *Radical Compassion: Shambhala Publications Authors on the Path of Boundless Love*. Boston, MA: Shambhala.

3. This quote has long been attributed to e.e. cummings, but the origin of it remains a mystery and consequently, there is some debate as to whether he actually ever said it.

4. Jinpa, Thupten. 2015. *A Fearless Heart: How the Courage to Be Compassionate Can Transform Our Lives*. New York: Avery.

5. The Dalai Lama. 2001. *An Open Heart: Practicing Compassion in Everyday Life*. New York: Little Brown and Company, p. 109.

6. Staats, Cheryl. 2016. "Understanding Implicit Bias: What Educators Should Know." *American Educator*, Winter 2015–2016: 29.

7. See, for example, Schaffer, Connie L., White, Meg, and Corine Meredith Brown. 2016. *Questioning Assumptions and Challenging Perceptions Becoming an Effective Teacher in Urban Environments*. Lanham, MD: Rowman & Littlefield.

8. See, for example, Greenwald, Anthony G., Mahzarin R. Banaji, Laurie A. Rudman, Shelly D. Farnham, Brian A. Nosek, and Deborah S. Mellott. 2002. "A Unified Theory of Implicit Attitudes, Stereotypes, Self-Esteem, and Self-Concept." *Psychological Review* 109(1): 3–25.

9. Whyte, David. 2015. *Consolations: The Solace, Nourishment and Underlying Meaning of Everyday Words*. Langley, WA: Many Rivers Press, p. 13.

10. Ambrose, Susan A., Michael W. Bridges, Michele DiPietro, Marsha C. Lovett, and Marie K. Norman. 2010. *How Learning Works: 7 Researched-Based Principles for Smart Teaching*. San Francisco, CA: Jossey-Bass.

11. Zakrzewski, Vicki. 2012. "How Self-Compassion Can Help Prevent Teacher Burnout." *Greater Good Magazine*, September 11. Retrieved May 23, 2017 (http://greatergood.berkeley.edu/article/item/self_compassion_for_teachers, para. 3).

12. Faculty Focus Special Report. 2017. *Mid-Career Faculty: How to Stay Engaged, Fulfilled and Productive*. Madison, WI: Magna Publications, p. 3.

13. McKee, Annie, and Kandi Wiens. 2017. "Prevent Burnout by Making Compassion a Habit." *Harvard Business Review*, May 11. Retrieved July 18, 2017 (https://hbr.org/2017/05/prevent-burnout-by-making-compassion-a-habit).

14. Neff, Kristen. 2015. *Self-Compassion: The Proven Power of Being Kind to Yourself*. New York: Morrow.

15. Kabat-Zinn, Jon. 2017. MBSR Training Online. Retrieved September 8, 2017 (http://www.mbsrtraining.com/about-jon-kabat-zinn/).

16. Neff, Kristen. N.d. "Self-Compassion." Self-Compassion.org. Retrieved May 23, 2017 (http://self-compassion.org/the-three-elements-of-self-compassion-2/).

17. Jennings, Patricia A., and Mark T. Greenberg. 2009. "The Prosocial Classroom: Teacher Social and Emotional Competence in Relation to Student and Classroom Outcomes." *Review of Educational Research* 79(1): 491–525. Jennings, Patricia A.,

Karin E. Snowberg, Michael A. Coccia, and Mark T. Greenberg. 2011. "Improving Classroom Learning Environments by Cultivating Awareness and Resilience in Education (CARE): Results of Two Pilot Studies." *Journal of Classroom Interaction* 46(1): 37–48. Roeser, Robert W., Ellen Skinner, Jeffry Beers, and Patricia A. Jennings. 2012. "Mindfulness Training and Teachers' Professional Development: An Emerging Area of Research and Practice." *Child Development Perspectives* 6(2): 167–173.

18. Quoted in Aguilar, Elena. 2016. "Just Breathe: When Teachers Practice Mindfulness." *Edutopia* (blog), May 27. Retrieved May 27, 2016 (http://www.edutopia .org/blog/just-breathe-when-teachers-practice-mindfulness-elena-aguilar, para. 6).

19. Zakrzewski, "How Self-Compassion Can Help Prevent Teacher Burnout," para. 3.

20. Neff, Kristen. n.d. "Self-Compassion: Tips for Practice." Self-Compassion .org. Retrieved July 20, 2017 (http://self-compassion.org/tips-for-practice/).

21. Seppala, Emma. 2015. "Why Compassion Is a Better Managerial Tactic Than Toughness." *Harvard Business Review*, May 7. Retrieved May 17, 2016 (https://hbr .org/2015/05/why-compassion-is-a-better-managerial-tactic-than-toughness).

CONCLUSION

1. Mills, C. Wright. 1958. *The Sociological Imagination*. New York: Oxford.

2. Christakis, Nicholas A., and James H. Fowler. 2011. *Connected: The Surprising Power of Our Social Networks and How They Shape Our Lives*. New York: Back Bay Books, p. xv.

3. Hanh, Thich Nhat. 2017. "The Practice of Sangha." *Lion's Roar*, July 7. Retrieved July 21, 2017 (https://www.lionsroar.com/the-practice-of-sangha/).

4. Wolpow, Ray, Mona M. Johnson, Ron Hertel, and Susan O. Kincaid. 2016. *The Heart of Learning and Teaching: Compassion, Resilience, and Academic Success.* Washington State Office of Superintendent of Public Instruction (OSPI) Compassionate Schools. Retrieved September 7, 2017 (http://www.k12.wa.us/compassionate schools/pubdocs/TheHeartofLearningandTeaching.pdf).

5. Rosenberg, Marshall. 2015. "Nonviolent Communication: A Language of Compassion." The Center for Nonviolent Communication. Retrieved September 8, 2017 (https://www.cnvc.org/Training/nvc-chapter-1).

Index

academic brutalization, 7

acceptance, x; guest house type of, 96; responsibility and, 47–50; vulnerability and, 50–52

acrostic poetry, 19–20

active learning, xi

administrators, 48

adversity: attending to, 33–34; investigation of, 34–36; as recognized, 31–32; students understood through, 27–28; transforming, 37; to understanding, 28–29; violence or injustice not condoned in, 128n16

altruism, 13

anger: body location of, 33; as compassion, 34, 41, 108; listening to our, 32; physical sensations in, 36

antiracism: classroom chemistry as, 65; *Everyday Antiracism: Getting Real about Race in Schools* (Dance), 15; resources for, 126n10

anxiety: oral presentations and, 17; stress resulting in, 9

Armstrong, Karen, xix, 97; Charter for Compassion from, xviii; on compassion born of interdependence, 67; on dethroning selves, 44; on

Golden Rule, 13; on inviolable sanctity of beings, 81–82; on treating with justice, 47

art, 85

Ashton, Marvin J., 27, 31

assertion: communication and, 39–40; ego authority and blind, 45

assessment measures: cheating on, 49; culturally responsive classrooms and, 59; time spent on, 18

assumptions, 6–8

attending, 32–34

beginner's mind: cup as emptied for, 1; knowledge mastering and, 22; learning and teaching exercise in, 3–4; learning from students as, 2; open mind from, 10; practicing, 92; teacher modeling, 3–4, 5, 9, 11; teachers with, 11

biases: overcoming, 104–9; self identification of, 114; welcoming checklist with, 60

blame: caution on, 111; destructive cycle of, 47–50; on students, 54

boundaries: compassion and holding space from, 91; negative and positive images of, 99; self-worth in, 52–53

Boyle, Gregory, 28

About the Authors

Peter Kaufman has been an educator for over twenty years. He is a professor of sociology at the State University of New York, New Paltz, where he teaches courses on introduction to sociology, education and society, social change, social interaction, and sociological theory. He has been a regular member of the editorial board of *Teaching Sociology* and is a recipient of the State University of New York Chancellor's Award for Excellence in Teaching. He lives in New Paltz, New York, with his wife, Leigh, and their greyhound, Billy.

Janine Schipper is a professor of sociology at Northern Arizona University where she writes about and teaches courses in environmental sociology and contemplative studies. She is the author of *Disappearing Desert: The Growth of Phoenix and the Culture of Sprawl* (University of Oklahoma Press, 2008) and "Toward a Buddhist Sociology: Its Theories, Methods and Possibilities" (*American Sociologist*, 2012). Janine is a guest teacher at the Flagstaff Insight Meditation Community and facilitates workshops on compassion and mindfulness practices. She lives in Flagstaff, Arizona, with her husband and three wild, beautiful children.

Made in the USA
Las Vegas, NV
26 July 2021